Prescription for Advertising

Rx for Advertising

Edmond A. Bruneau

BOSTON BOOKS

Second Printing

PRESCRIPTION FOR ADVERTISING. Copyright © 1986 by Edmond A. Bruneau. All rights reserved. Printed in the United States of America. No part of this book may be used or reproduced in any manner without written permission, except in the case of brief quotations embodied in critical articles and reviews. For information address Boston Books, P.O. Box 9909, Spokane, Washington 99209-0909.

A special thanks to Marla Leander, who designed both the cover and inside pages; Shaun Higgins, who patiently contributed his editing skills; and Typesetting Unlimited — especially Linda G. Watkins — whose careful dedication to the typeset word matches the goodwill inside their hearts.

Library of Congress Cataloging in Publication Data

Bruneau, Edmond A., 1953 —
    Prescription for advertising.
    A Common Sense Cure for Business Owners & Managers
    1. Advertising   2. Business   I. Title

LC Class: HF5823   **Dewey:** 659.1   **LC Card #:** 86-71075

ISBN 0-9616683-1-8 (Hardbound)
ISBN 0-9616683-2-6 (Paperback)

*This book is dedicated
to my wife, Susan Marie,
who helped make this book possible
with her love, patience and encouragement.*

Few things are as common as common sense.
— **Kin Hubbard**

In business, the competition will bite you if you keep running; if you stand still, they will swallow you.
— **William S. Knudsen**
  Former Chairman of General Motors

Introduction

Why I Wrote This Book

There are few books that attempt to explain what a business really should know about advertising. Now, there's at least one.

A lot of business people have tried to find books on practical advertising fundamentals. Unfortunately, they usually get the wrong book.

Many advertising books are written by college professors who are predictably academic. These books are important for students who are studying advertising as a profession, but don't furnish the business owner or manager what he really needs to know. Topics are covered such as . . . the history of advertising; social implications; leaders in advertising; applications to behavioral science, etc., etc.

These type of books are often strong in advertising theory and rather weak in application. That's because "Ivory Tower" authors often lack real practical experience.

Another category of advertising books that are usually

the "wrong kind" are written by advertising professionals.

Usually written by retired advertising agency presidents or vice-presidents, the authors talk about how wonderful the business was to them, the funny clients they encountered, stories about famous advertising figures and other experiences in the wacky world of advertising. These books are fun to read, but don't do much for the business that has to advertise in today's competitive environment.

However, there are a few books written by advertising people that *do* have a lot of value. Books by David Ogilvy, George Lois, John Caples, Jack Trout and Al Ries and others make significant points about the business and are worth reading and learning from.

Trouble is, such books are too often written for advertising people, not for the typical businessperson. These books also tend to concentrate on only certain portions of the advertising business . . . such as Positioning, Advertising Production, Media Buying, Creativity, etc.

That's why I decided to write this book. Business people need a handbook they can refer to before making crucial advertising decisions.

But this book is *not* a "how-to-create-advertising" book.

It is a *"highly-opinionated"* comprehensive guide for working within the mechanisms of advertising which already exist. Many professionals in the advertising business may not agree with my advice. You may not either. That's okay.

This book *will* help you become aware of the options that exist in the advertising business . . . and show you ways to get the most return on your advertising investment.

The following pages attempt to answer some of the questions which occur when a business peers into the mysterious universe of advertising. It is written in an easy-to-understand way . . . and it includes information and suggestions *you can use*.

"Should I hire an artist or let the newspaper create my ad?" "How do I know a good radio schedule from a bad one?" "Should I do my advertising in-house or hire outside help?" "How should I pay my advertising agency?"

These questions and more are discussed and answered in the chapters ahead. The purpose of this book is to give you a better understanding of how advertising can work for you . . . and how to manage it successfully.

Hopefully, after reading this book, advertising won't be so strange. More than likely, you'll avoid a lot of problems and save wasted time and money.

Better yet, by managing your advertising investment in a practical manner, your profits *will* increase.

And making money is the bottom line in any investment, isn't it?

TABLE OF CONTENTS

Introduction
Why I Wrote this Book vi

Chapter One
Seeing the Whole Elephant 1

Chapter Two
Getting Where You Want To Go 4

Chapter Three
Creativity — The Power to Break Through 8

Chapter Four
Setting an Advertising Budget 12

Chapter Five
**The Choice of Advertising Internally
or Using an Outside Agency** 19

Chapter Six
Finding a Good Advertising Agency 26

Chapter Seven
Setting the Ground Rules with Your Agency 31

Chapter Eight
How to Pay Your Advertising Agency 36

Chapter Nine
Keeping Your Agency on the Right Track 45

Chapter Ten
How to Work with Your Account Executive 49

Chapter Eleven
How to Work with a Writer 54

Chapter Twelve
How to Work with an Artist 61

Chapter Thirteen
How to Work with a Photographer 66

Chapter Fourteen
Why Media Planning and Buying Is So Important 75

Chapter Fifteen
How to Buy Print Advertising 80

Chapter Sixteen
How to Buy Effective Radio 87

Chapter Seventeen
The Lure of Television 95

Chapter Eighteen
Advertising on Billboards, Buses and Benches 101

Chapter Nineteen
Signs — the Other Outdoor Advertising Medium 105

Chapter Twenty
Reaching Your Prospects Through the Mail 113

Chapter Twenty-one
Specialty Advertising 120

Chapter Twenty-two
It Pays to Co-operate with CO-OP Advertising 125

Chapter Twenty-three
How to Work with Printers 129

Chapter Twenty-four
Logo Lament 135

Chapter Twenty-five
Newsletters, Another Way to Advertise 139

Chapter Twenty-six
How to Write a Press Release 142

Chapter Twenty-seven
Creating Unconventional Convention Displays 147

Chapter Twenty-eight
Avoid a Romance with Research 152

Chapter Twenty-nine
Advertising: The Challenge of Blazing New Trails 157

Chapter Thirty
Knowing Enough to be Dangerous 161

Sometimes it is more important to discover what one cannot do, than what one can do.
— *Lin Yutang*

Everyone lives by selling something.
— *Robert Louis Stevenson*

Chapter One

Seeing the Whole Elephant

There's a short tale about three blind men describing what their impression of an elephant was.

The first one felt its tail and said the elephant was like a rope. The second touched its trunk and concluded that the elephant must be like a big snake. The third blind man put his arms around one of its feet and explained that an elephant was like a tree.

Sometimes people tend to look at advertising in the same way.

I once talked to a businessman who explained to me that he didn't believe in advertising because he tried it before and it didn't work. "It didn't do my business any good," he said.

"What kind of advertising did you do?" I asked.

"TV," he growled. "Cost a lot of money, too."

So I listened. A television station salesman had told him about the power of television and how it could pull in hundreds of people into his small little store. Knowing the store owner didn't have a lot of money, he said that his station could produce a TV commercial at minimum cost. And he had a list of programs that weren't expensive to buy time on at all.

The store owner thought the offer sounded pretty good. So, he bought the time, had the station make the commercial spot and spent the money.

And hundreds of people *didn't* flock into his business. "So, you see, advertising doesn't work for my store," he concluded.

There is a saying that goes something like . . . "If a cat jumps on a hot stove, it won't do it again." Now that makes a lot of sense for cats, but humans, as intelligent as we are, sometimes turn that stove into a giant furnace.

The same scenario could have happened to the store owner trying advertising with any other media, not just television. He might have even had an advertising agency do some work for him. And he might have come to the same conclusion.

So, why advertise? Easy. You advertise for profit. You advertise for a stronger image. You advertise to succeed. No matter if you're running a political campaign or a grocery store down the street, advertising is the best method I know to influence behavior.

The problem with that poor store owner is that he didn't understand advertising in the first place. He trusted the television station salesman, who was probably trying to dump some programs on him that he couldn't fill.

And the store owner *didn't* think about a lot of things. Who is my audience? Is television the right advertising medium? Is my commercial on the programs that reach my audience? How will they perceive my commercial? Am I spending enough to be effective? What kind of results do I need in order for my advertising to be a good investment?

He just saw part of the elephant.

As you can see, there are some basic things to learn about advertising before any buying decisions are made, anywhere. This book will attempt to give you a better picture of the elephant.

Advertising is never a guaranteed commodity. There are just too many factors that can influence the job advertising has to do. But the bet can be hedged by knowing what *not* to do.

Advertising does work. That's why it exists. The trick is to do it the same way you make any important business decision . . . carefully.

Buying a pig-in-a-poke, like that poor store owner did, is a real good way to be soured on advertising.

No matter if you deal with the media direct or hire an advertising agency, you still should be acquainted with the principles in the following chapters.

You know your own business hopefully better than anyone else. By knowing more about advertising, you'll be able to understand more about why things are done the way they're done. A combination of those two things leads to better communication with the advertisers.

And that will benefit you and your business.

In new business, if you engage in anything short of a direct assault on the jugular vein, you're in the Mickey Mouse league.
— **William Holden**

Success comes in cans, failure in can'ts.
— **Bits & Pieces**

Chapter Two

Getting Where You Want To Go

Before you advertise, think about your business. *How* do you want your public to think about you? *Where* do you want to be next year? In five years?

The way you portray your image in advertising has a lot to do with the way your prospects think about you.

And in turn, the way your prospects think about you has a lot to do with who you really are.

This concept is called many things . . . the term most popular today is *Positioning*. By successfully *positioning* your business where you want it to be in your prospects' mind, you eventually achieve that position.

Now, it may sound simple. But there are thousands of businesses who never even think about *what* they are and *where* they want to be before beginning advertising efforts. They are thinking only about selling products or services.

But the fact of the matter is, when you attempt to

influence people to buy, you are also selling yourself in the process.

Let's pretend that two stores with similar clothing merchandise go into business, both at convenient locations. Their chance of survival is equal.

One store, let's say Store X, is careful and smart. Its owners know that their clothing lines are aimed at teens and that being the "in" place to go is the position Store X needs to achieve. Clothing is marked at retail, displayed well and they hire student leaders to work in the store part time. They sponsor fashion shows at schools and when they advertise, they advertise the look of the new fashions in an avant-garde, "hot-look" way. Store X positions itself as a hot, "in" store in everything they do, including their advertising. And Store X makes money.

Now Store Y sees things differently. Its owners want to give teenagers a break from the high cost of fashions. So they take the position of a discount store. The store lacks a fancy layout, is mostly self-service, and just has cashiers running the store. Store Y advertises low prices. No hot theme. Just a plain look and lots of prices in their ads. In time, Store Y can't afford as many ads as Store X because it didn't make as much money on the merchandise. "But why would people pay more for the same clothes at a more expensive place?"

In a matter of months, Store Y has a "going-out-of-business" sale. Why? Because the *position* it chose didn't coincide with the market it was trying to reach. And no thought of the positioning was applied to its advertising. The plain advertising approach may have worked well for other products or other markets. But it didn't work for teenage clothing.

When teenage prospects were asked what the difference was between the two stores, they explained that Store X was a fun place to go, it had an excellent selection and that the people were very knowledgeable about fashion. Store Y, they believed, sold less-than-quality merchandise and name brand seconds in order to offer discount prices. Some never saw or heard the ads. Many never had been to Store Y.

Obviously, what they believed about Store Y wasn't even true. But now that Store Y is out-of-business, it doesn't really matter, does it?

How you *position* your business is vital to its success. Store Y had a good idea . . . and handled differently, the store might still be selling clothing today.

You cannot position your business in a place where your market won't accept it.

That's why it's so important to think about who you are . . . who your market is . . . and what you'd like to become in your prospects' mind.

Your positioning should determine your business name, your advertising image . . . and the places that you advertise.

Ego plays a detrimental part in the demise of many companies Owners think they "know" who they are, yet continue to misrepresent their business image in their advertising . . . usually because their eyes see only the hard work and sacrifice it has taken to make their business what it is. The trick is to see your business through the buyers' eyes, instead.

If your prospects think of you differently than the way you perceive yourself, you've got a positioning problem. Store Y thought it was a discount store. To its prospects, Store Y was a store that lacked quality.

Getting Where You Want to Go

The best way to learn how your prospects perceive you is to get outside opinions. Not from your assistant or any other employee. They value their jobs, remember?

Advertising agencies and marketing consultants often use "Focus Groups" . . . a group of outside people brought together to discuss a variety of topics about your industry. If properly directed, you could find out a lot about your business image without the participants even knowing who was sponsoring the session.

The point is that advertising can help you do more than sell products and services. It can build your image. And it can position your firm in a manner that will attract more business than before.

So, *before you start to advertise,* think about your positioning. Then make your advertising fit the position you want. Appeal to the right audience in the right way. If your ads don't represent the way you are — or at least the way you should be — change them.

Store Y didn't understand about how advertising applied to its positioning. And Store Y probably doesn't believe in advertising anymore.

But Store X does.

The most dangerous kind of advertising anyone can run today is "safe advertising" . . . "Safe advertising" that looks . . . so familiar, so conventional, so reassuring, that it is actually invisible to the consumer. So while "safe advertising" may seem appropriate — on the surface — the impact that it fails to deliver in the marketplace makes "safe advertising" about as dangerous as you can get.
— *John Ferrell*
  Executive VP, Creative Director
  Young & Rubicam

Chapter Three

Creativity — The Power to Break Through

How many advertisements is the normal person subject to everyday? Hundreds. Maybe even more. Studies indicate the average person is subject to 600 to 1,600 advertising messages a day.

During an average morning, you probably have seen at least 50 ads in your newspaper . . . listened to 30 commercials on the radio . . . passed 20 billboards and who knows how many business signs. And it's not even 9:00 a.m. yet.

But now it's 9:05 a.m. and you're sitting at your desk. How many of those advertisements do you remember? Ten? Five? None? That's no surprise. On an average, only one out of sixteen messages can be recalled.

With so many advertisements bombing your brain every morning, is it any wonder that you've built up a "tune-out" psychological defense? There's no way your

Creativity

brain can remember them all, so it simply shuts most of them out.

At least 80% of advertising that's done today is not even worth remembering. So, let's talk about the other 20%. The stuff that breaks through the barrier of boredom — the only type of advertising that's worth doing.

It doesn't make sense to buy space or time for an advertisement that no one remembers. If your advertising doesn't stand out among the hundreds of commercials people are exposed to, it's just going to be part of the blur. And whatever message it carried is going to miss your prospect's brain.

And the purpose is to hit the brain with your message, isn't it?

That's where creativity comes in. Properly used, creativity can be the rocket that thrusts its way through your prospects' protective barrier. Your advertising reaches them so they can *remember* your message. Then it has a chance to work.

Does creativity mean bizarre? Strange? Far out? Sometimes. But usually it means simply a surprise.

When all the ads look the same in the newspaper, the one that looks a little different, or has something different to say, is a nice surprise. And it gets read.

The TV commercial that doesn't treat a beer commercial like a beer commercial is a nice surprise. It gets watched. A radio spot that brings in a touch of humor is a nice surprise. And people listen. In every other type of advertising, the same is true. A creative approach gets attention.

Almost anyone can write an advertisement about their business or products or services. But unless you are

Creativity

a creative person, it's just not going to be very interesting. And if it isn't interesting, you're back in the 80% pile of uselessness. It's amazing that so many advertisers create dull, mediocre advertising. But they do.

In a way, that's good . . . because when you create a good, creative, interesting advertisement, it only competes with the attention people are giving the other 20%.

If the quality of advertisements start to get better and the percentages of interesting advertisements increase, you'll have to figure out another way to break through the brain barrier. But don't worry. It probably won't happen.

So, you want your advertisements to be creative, but the question is how, right?

The answer is simple: Hire a creative person or group to help you. I don't know why, but a lot of people find it difficult to hire someone to come up with a creative concept and then let them execute the concept with copy, art and/or photography.

Would you represent yourself in court? Or work on your own teeth? Or perform a song? That's what lawyers, dentists and musicians are for. Creating creative advertising is what artists, consultants and advertising agencies are for.

Not all of them will have "the right stuff." There are some lawyers who frankly are not very good. For the most part, though, you'll take a giant step toward good advertising when you look in the Yellow Pages and get professional help. Creative help, that is.

These "creative" people come up with interesting concepts for a living. Most of the time, they're pretty good at it, too. If you think about it, it's a tough job to come up with advertising approaches people will find interesting day after day. But that's their talent.

By using creative people, you have a lot better chance to get into that 20% bracket that gets noticed.

When they return with an idea that makes you want to say "No one advertises like *that*," or "That's an awfully unusual approach," or "I think it's crap" . . . hold your tongue for a minute and ask them to explain how it's going to work. And listen hard.

You might be judging the advertisement by standards you developed by seeing other advertisements. And that's not the right way to judge creativity.

A lot of creative people complain that they create new, interesting ideas that no one has seen before . . . and then the client doesn't like them because he doesn't feel "comfortable" with the new ideas.

If your creative people can explain how the *surprise* of the advertising is going to capture audience interest . . . and still sell the aspects of your message, you may have some real winners, even if their ideas seem a little strange right now.

Applying creativity to your advertising is the best way of increasing your chances of being remembered. And that means greater effectiveness.

Methods of locating the right "creative" help for you will be discussed in upcoming chapters.

Advertising is too expensive to waste. Remember, dull ads work in dull ways. Interesting ads get attention and are remembered. Which kind can you afford?

HOW TO BURY A GOOD IDEA
It will never work.
We've never done it that way before.
We're doing fine without it.
We can't afford it.
We're not ready for it.
It's not our responsibility.
— Bits & Pieces

Chapter Four

Setting An Advertising Budget

The first thing a business usually tells me when I try to help them set up an advertising budget is "I don't see why a budget is really necessary."

The second thing they say is "that's way too much money."

When you create an advertising budget, you create a tool that helps you live within your means. It helps you make economical, rather than emotional decisions. It provides expense figures that can be evaluated against results. And it helps keep you from starving yourself.

That's right . . . starving. You see, most businesses have no idea how much their advertising budget should be. They *do know*, however, that it should be kept to a minimum, at all costs. Ha. And that's why they starve. And that's probably why they can't set a good budget. Bad advertising budget attitude.

I once worked with a client who had a set advertising budget, but squawked when I created a media plan to spend it. I asked him, "Don't you want to spend all the amount you've allowed?" "Not if I can help it," he replied.

Now if you fall in the "Not if I can help it" category, this chapter may do you absolutely no good at all. Because a budget isn't a true budget unless it's used.

Somewhere along the way, business managers got the idea that they could "save money" by spending less than they planned to in advertising. That doesn't say much for their planning in the first place, does it?

When you create an amount of money to spend on advertising, it should be determined as precisely as possible, based upon several concerns . . .

1. The sales levels you want to achieve.
2. The profit you want to make.
3. How much competition you have for your prospect's attention.
4. The position you want to create in your market.

Unless those considerations change, cutting the planned budget back is simply saying "We don't want as many sales as we planned for," or "Even though there are 15 lawnmower ads in the paper today, people will choose our smaller one,"or "Being a stylish, with-it clothing store to teenagers isn't important. Our prices are what matters." (See Chapter 2).

In other words, there's no magic in budgets. No rabbit in the hat. You can't expect to cut back your budget and maintain your goals.

So set a solid budget in the first place and live by it. If, after a year passed, you couldn't fill the orders, cut

Setting an Advertising Budget

it back. If it increased your business 10 percent and you really wanted to increase 20 percent, increase it.

If you are into your advertising program for three or four months and are simply not getting the results you expected, you may want to increase your budget right away. Adjusting a budget that was set too low makes a lot more sense than trying to justify the original budget and "sticking to it, no matter what."

Maybe you can see now that a budget *is* necessary. So let's talk about money before we go any further.

The cost of advertising is no bargain. It's an expense. Sometimes a pretty large expense, too. And many times it's hard to see immediate results. But most good investments fall into the same category.

I once lost a client by comparing his advertising to the investment in the new building he just built. He didn't want to set a logical budget for advertising and could only "afford" a certain small amount. So I looked outside at the building being constructed and said, "How can you afford to build a new facility?" He was stunned.

"A building is a long term investment," I explained, "and it requires a certain amount of money to build it. And in the end, it will probably pay off. But if you cheapen the labor and materials, you won't get the building you need. Your advertising investment is the same thing. Base it on a realistic plan and provide the money it takes to do it and it will probably pay off."

Well, again I was told the amount he allotted was all his business could afford. "Then don't spend it until you have enough," I said.

He didn't listen. His business created their own "in-house" advertising (to save money, of course) and spent the money "they could afford." Result? Bad advertising without enough power behind it to penetrate the market . . . and they can't make the payments on their new building anymore. He shot himself in the foot.

The point is, the amount you spend is relative to what you want to achieve. Not what you think you can afford. And it may seem like a lot of money. But if you get the results you want, it was well worth it. If you don't get the results you want, you should re-examine all the elements of your advertising, like positioning, creativity, production and media buy. The problem may even be in the product or service you're selling.

One of the main reasons why some people don't believe in advertising is that they didn't ever provide enough money to do the job in the first place.

Setting the proper advertising budget is one of the most important and serious jobs a business owner or manager does.

My advice? Every year, sit down and make solid plans on the three points mentioned earlier. Then take a look at your advertising budget and put enough money in it to accomplish your goals.

Different businesses spend different percentages of their annual sales goals on advertising. So how much *should* you allow?

The most basic way is to figure out what you expect your annual gross sales (not net) will be and take a percentage based upon the traditional percentage used for your type of business.

The following chart may help.

Setting an Advertising Budget

Advertising Budget in Relation to Gross Sales

MANUFACTURING
Agriculture	0.40
Mining	0.23
Oil	0.42
Home Construction Contractors	1.00
Commercial Construction Contractors	0.26
Associated Service Contractors	1.38
Food	3.24
Tobacco	6.79
Dairy Products	2.31
Bakery Products	2.10
Beverages	5.96
Textiles - Weaving & Knitting	1.11
Carpet and Rug Mills	0.92
Apparel/Clothing	1.29
Furs	3.68
Logging, Sawmills, Millwork	0.47
Prefab Buildings & Mobile Homes	1.87
Household Furniture	2.14
Office Furniture	1.95
Pulp & Paper Mills	1.33
Paperboard Containers & Boxes	0.85
Newspaper Publishing	1.07
Periodical Publishing	1.02
Commercial Printing	1.83
Greeting Card Publishing	4.12
Chemical Manufacturers	3.21
Petroleum Refining	1.21
Tire Manufacturers	2.34
Plastic Products	1.76
Leather Products	2.07
Stone, Clay & Glass Manufacturing	0.87
Metal Refining & Forming	0.93
Metal Cans & Shipping Containers	1.41
Cutlery, Hand Tools & Hardware	4.22
Other Metal Fabricated Products	0.89
Engines & Turbines	0.97
Farm & Garden Equipment	1.33
Special Industrial Machinery	1.11
General Industrial Machinery	1.28
Service Industry Machinery	1.49
Electric Industrial Apparatus	1.19
Household Appliances	2.35
Radio & TV Receiving Equipment	3.60
Computers and Peripherals	3.41
Motor Vehicles & Equipment	1.23
Aircraft & Parts	0.35
Transportation Equipment other than Motor Vehicles	2.30
Engineering & Scientific Instruments	2.86
Measuring & Controlling Instruments	1.67
Optical Instruments & Lenses	4.23
Photographic Equipment & Supplies	2.77
Watches, Clocks & Parts	5.17
Jewelry, Silverware	3.62
Musical Instruments	2.33
Toys, Amusements & Sporting Goods	4.89
Railroads	0.21
Local & Suburban Passenger Transportation	0.84
Local & Long Distance Hauling	0.39
Air Transportation	3.17
Pipe Lines	0.09

COMMUNICATIONS
Telephone Companies	1.84
Radio & TV Broadcasting	1.19

UTILITIES
Electric Services	0.49
Gas Production & Distribution	0.45

WHOLESALERS
Motor Vehicles & Automotive Parts	0.97
Furniture & Home Furnishings	1.68
Lumber & Construction Materials	0.19
Electrical Goods	0.79
Hardware, Plumbing & Heating Equipment	0.42
Paper & Paper Products	0.21

Setting an Advertising Budget

Drugs & Drug Store Supplies	0.61
Apparel, Footwear & Notions	0.51
Groceries and Related Products	0.44
Petroleum & Related Products	0.43
Beer, Wine & Alcoholic Beverages	0.67

RETAILERS

Lumber & Building Supplies	0.91
Department Stores	2.81
General Merchandise Stores	3.11
Grocery Stores	1.55
Automobiles	1.29
Gasoline Service Stations	1.07
Boat Dealers	1.36
Trailer Dealers	1.27
Clothing Stores	2.66
Furniture & Home Furnishing Stores	3.83
Eating & Drinking Places	2.14
Liquor Stores	0.71
Misc. Retailers	1.37

FINANCE

Banks, Savings & Loans	2.04
Personal Credit Institutions	2.66
Business Credit Institutions	0.71

INSURANCE

Title Insurance	0.47
Insurance Agents & Brokers	1.92

INVESTMENT

Real Estate Agents/Managers	1.73
Investment, Security, Broker Firms	1.55

SERVICES

Hotels, Lodging Facilities	2.84
Personal Services	1.97
Business Services	1.69
Advertising Agencies	2.10
Automotive Rental & Leasing	0.81
Automotive Repair Shops	0.93
Electrical Repair Shops	1.20
Motion Picture Production	3.72
Motion Picture Theatres	6.89
Misc. Amusements, Sports & Recreation	3.49
Nursing & Personal Care Facilities	0.48
Hospitals	0.71
Medical & Dental Laboratories	0.17
Engineering & Architectural Services	0.31
Accounting Firms	0.40

This chart was compiled from a multitude of sources, including a national advertising magazine and various industry newsletters. It is intended as guideline for different types of businesses and should be adjusted accordingly per each individual application.

Setting an Advertising Budget

Before you set your budget, keep in mind the following:

A.) A small business advertising budget usually requires a bigger percentage of sales than a similar larger business. Advertising simply spreads a little further if a business has more than one outlet.

B.) "Launching" a new product or business (introducing it to the marketplace) requires a lot more money than is needed for promoting an established product. Someone once said that an aircraft uses a major part of its fuel just to get off the ground. That's something to keep in mind when you budget.

C.) If you have a lot of competition, you may have to spend more money to reach the mind of your prospect. That's because you have to compete for the limited attention your prospect gives to advertising in the first place.

D.) When you position your business as the leader in the area, you want to add new customers and steal established customers from your competition. Remember that adding market share is an expensive proposition . . . because it takes more than ordinary advertising to convince people to switch. Make sure you supplement your budget accordingly.

Setting goals and a solid advertising budget is a significant step toward making advertising work for you.
Next is figuring out what to do . . . and how to do it.

Highly creative people are often off their rockers.
— **Stanley Hoffmann**

We have met the enemy and they is us.
— **Walt Kelly**
  Pogo

Chapter Five

The Choice of Using In-House Talent or Working With an Outside Agency
The In-House/Out-House Dilemma

Deciding where and how to do your advertising is one of the most eternal questions in business. And one of the most critical, too.

After all, such a decision determines the seed you plant. But what a lot of people forget is that it also determines how it grows.

Frankly, I'm no fan of in-house advertising agencies. I worked in one for over five years.

The basic assumption when I was there was that performing advertising in-house saved money. That assumption was sadly mistaken.

You see, most of the time, the idea of doing advertising in-house comes from an overzealous employee or

Advertising Internally or Outside

manager who claims that he or she can "save the company a lot of money."

When money is discussed, people listen. Financial directors listen. The company president listens. "Advertising is such an expense anyway, why should we pay an outside firm all that money when we could do it ourselves for far less? We could save money on art, creative time and collect our own commissions. And it would be better because we wouldn't have to argue with those crazy agency people all the time."

Such is the point-of-view from the inside. Notice that quality and results are not the first criteria. Saving money is.

And that's where the logic drives me crazy.

Let's unravel the argument by starting with the statement *"Advertising is such an expense anyway . . ."* Somewhere along the line, some people left out advertising as a legitimate cost of doing business. It's no different from the high cost of materials, rent or labor. And just like all those other factors, the quality of what you buy is just as important as the price you pay for it.

So unless the quality is the same, paying less is no bargain.

Next is: *"Why should we pay an outside firm all that money when we could do it ourselves for far less?"*

Let me put it this way. Perhaps you're in the insurance business. Or the clothing business. Or the hardware business. Or the computer business. It's hard enough to consistently be good at the business you're already in. Why spend a portion of your time and energy pursuing another business that must compete against people who do it full time?

If you're in the clothing business, it doesn't make sense to go into the computer business just because you need a computer, does it?

So why does it make sense to go into the advertising business because you need to advertise? Especially when you have to compete with full time professionals in everything you do.

The temptation is greater because it looks so easy. It's "just" some copy. "Just" a photograph. "Just" some art. "Just" a media plan.

And if you really believe it's all "just" that easy to create great advertising, go into the business full time yourself. But don't try to do it halfway.

Here comes the funny part. *"We could save money on art, creative time and collect our own commissions."* The basic premise of a good advertising agency is that it pays the cost of great talent and shares a *portion* of those costs with each of its clients.

So, it doesn't make a lot of sense to pull in a Creative Director who makes $75,000 to $150,000 a year into an in-house agency, or the same caliber of artists, writers, production people, marketing people and media people. That wouldn't be "saving money."

The in-house agency does one of two things. It either creates an "affordable staff" consisting of lower paid people who wear many hats or attempts to utilize freelancers for what can't be handled in-house.

Now the "affordable staff" is an expense that companies should figure into the advertising costs. How much do those employees really cost you, in terms of benefits, insurance, salary, etc.? And then ask the hardest question. Why aren't they working where they could be making double the money in an advertising agency? Perhaps they're younger. Less experienced. Or not as capable.

Maybe they really aren't the people who should be at the helm of your company's future.

The "freelancer" approach works better . . . but most businesses cut corners and end up doing a halfway job. "We can't do the art, but I've got a 35mm camera," or "I know the company inside and out, so I'll write the copy," or "You make the ad, we'll buy the media," or "Anybody can do paste-up."

Get the idea? When corners are cut to save money, quality suffers. If you're not a professional photographer, don't assume you can take as good a picture. If you're not an advertising copywriter, don't assume you can write as well. And if you're not a professional artist, don't design the ad.

Some companies successfully hire freelancers to create advertising. But they do it for quality, not cost savings. It's a lot of work to find the right people to work on a project . . . and supervise them so it gets done right. When all the costs are added up, a business *can* save some money using freelance help instead of using an advertising agency. But it's a risk. Because there will always be things about the advertising business that an agency knows and you don't.

Remember that keeping up with all the advertising trends, styles, approaches, media changes, production technologies, etc., is a full-time job.

A good example is found when dealing directly with the media. Talk to any good newspaper salesperson and they'll tell you that print is the best way to advertise. But a television salesperson will chart the advantages of TV commercials. That's their job.

An agency works with all the media almost every day. Your agency can create a media plan that utilizes the right media in the right manner so that it works the best for you.

The final portion of the in-house argument went something like *". . . and it would be better because we wouldn't have to argue with those crazy agency people all the time."* Believe it or not, this is the strongest case *against* an in-house agency.

Those "crazy" agency people *should* be giving you an outside perspective of your business. If they believe you're seeing your situation from a personal or internal perspective, they *should* argue with you. Their out-of-house view of your business is one of the most important things they provide.

You can learn a lot about how other people, including your agency, perceive you, just by listening. They might be right, you know.

However, if you want "Yes" people . . . people who agree with you on most everything, then hire some in-house people to do your advertising. You won't get many arguments from people whose livelihood depends on your opinion of them.

If they see you going in the wrong direction, are they going to say, "Boss, this is a stupid idea"? If more money is needed to do the job right, but budgets have to be cut, will the in-house person be affected by how he'll look in the next financial report. You bet.

Advertising is not a calm, gentle business. It's a whirlwind of ideas, attitudes and creative talent going at gale

Advertising Internally or Outside

force. There's almost always a conflict of opinion. And those different opinions have to be discussed, sometimes even debated, if great advertising is to survive.

An in-house agency, just by its own survival, lets most of the wind out of the bag. And a lot of effective, powerful advertising is blown away.

They say getting Congress to cut its budget is a little bit like getting a pig to butcher itself. In a manner of speaking, an in-house agency is the same, but sometimes it will butcher your business first.

It's just easier and probably more efficient to rely on an agency that keeps up on all those things and provides you with top-notch creative, marketing, production and media assistance. Your time can then be focused on the most important aspect. Quality advertising that will bring results.

Most advertising agencies *are* full service. It's the "One Stop Shopping" concept. In other words, the agency can provide the marketing, creative, art, broadcast production, media buying . . . everything it takes to create good advertising.

The reason I bring this up is that some companies have successfully used agencies that are not full service. They utilize the creative and account services the agency provides and try to do the marketing and media buying themselves.

If you have simple marketing goals and very basic media buys, this may not be a bad route to follow. I do not recommend it for most applications, however. Buying media is often more complicated than people think . . . and the agency can often negotiate a lot better than the client can.

You should have an advertising agency for many reasons, but one of the foremost is utilizing its expertise. Another is that it can save you time. It doesn't make a whole lot of sense to use just part of an agency's experience, skill and talent and then spend extra time on your own part trying to do an element of the job by yourself. You won't save a lot of money and you probably won't do the job as well.

I believe that watching advertising costs is important. In fact, a future chapter is dedicated to getting the most from your agency at a fair price. Other upcoming chapters in this book are about working with different advertising media and different types of talent. They are written for two reasons. The first is for the business that is very small and *must* do some advertising on its own. The second is for a guideline. Even if you *do* work with an agency, you should know something about how different media are approached. And you should know how to best work with the talent within the agency. That's part of good agency/advertising management.

I really don't believe that becoming your own advertising agency in order to save money is the intelligent answer. Like anything else, there are exceptions to the rule.

But the cost of advertising is relative to its results. Get the best professionals you can to work on your advertising and you'll hedge the success of your investment.

Experience is knowing a lot of things you shouldn't do.
— *William S. Knudsen*

No corporation is hit by the future between the eyes; it's hit in the temple.
— *Joel Barker*
   President
   Infinity Ltd.

Chapter Six

Finding a Good Advertising Agency

You know what you want: You want an advertising agency that is very creative, but has a balanced marketing ability; a good track record with other clients; and one that doesn't overcharge for its services.

In short, an advertising agency that will make you money.

The question is, *how do you find one?*

It seems like everyone has a different approach. One business I know put "the word out on the street" by calling a few media people who encounter a lot of agencies. The hungry agencies in the area rapidly picked up the scent.

Another business used the "eenie-meenie-minie-moe" technique in the phone book.

Still another hired the first agency that made an unsolicited call at his door.

These are not methods I would recommend. However, here is an approach that I think works well.

Finding a Good Advertising Agency

First, gather a list of five agencies that you would consider as possibilities. These are agencies that maybe were suggested by business associates, have a good reputation in the area or have tried to call on you before you really became interested. Call them directly and ask the agency manager if they currently are handling a business like yourself. (If you're a bank, ask them if they currently are handling a financial institution, etc.)

If they're not, the agency is on your review list. If they are, tell them you would like to consider them in an upcoming agency review, but your policy is not to hire an agency with a duplicate account. Some agencies may see your business as a better opportunity and choose to tell you that they would drop their existing account if you hired them. If they so choose, add them to your list, too. After all, that agency's learning curve about a competitive product or business could come in quite handy.

So, after this process is finished, you should have at least three agencies on your review list. What a lot of companies do at this point is to ask for a presentation from each one of them.

Unfortunately, what usually happens is that the presentations are difficult to compare because the approach, money spent and the subject matter is so diverse.

I believe in comparing apples to apples. So, before you request a presentation, define a project . . . one that you know you'll be needing in the following months. On a piece of paper, type out some background on your company/product and any other details that could be helpful. If you can, define a budget for the project.

Then give all the agencies the same project, with the

Finding a Good Advertising Agency

same parameters and the same budget, and ask them for a proposal presentation. Tell them you will pay each for their out-of-pocket expenses, backed up by receipts. (If you want, you may want to put a maximum limit on that expense, too.) In addition, tell them you want a detailed list of what the work they did internally would have cost . . . and an estimate of production costs for going ahead with their proposal.

The reason I think you should pay for out-of-pocket proposal expenses is because it more equally compares the rich agencies and the less-rich. A rich agency is just one that's making more money . . . and charging more money . . . than the rest. It may not be better.

Schedule one presentation a day, and review each with someone with whom you can discuss the presentation's merits and minuses, such as a partner or assistant. Larger businesses may want to have a lot more people reviewing the presentations, but my advice is to keep reviewers at a minimum.

Listen carefully to each presentation. Ask questions. If an agency *did not* follow your guidelines . . . by spending more money than indicated or getting off the project subject or simply choosing to do it in a whole different way, be polite and say goodbye when it's finished. Then throw that agency's name away.

Even if it is comprised of the most charming people in the world, an agency that can't follow directions will not be an asset to your business.

Though the temptation is great, if the first presentation is the best you've ever seen, don't cancel the rest. After each presentation, use a rating system like the one below. It will compare the presentations in a fair, unemotional way.

Finding a Good Advertising Agency

PROPOSAL RATING SYSTEM

Agency: _____
Date: _____

1. Between 1-10, rate the creative approach the agency came up with for the new project.
2. Between 1-10, rate how well they justified *why* this approach should be taken.
3. Between 1-10, rate how well the agency chose media and spent the media budget you allocated.
4. Between 1-10, rate how well the proposal was presented.
5. Between 1-10, rate how well the agency understood and answered your questions.
6. Between 1-10, rate how fair you thought the internal costs and out-of-pocket costs were.
7. Between 1-10, rate how fair you thought the estimated production costs were.
8. Between 1-10, rate how balanced the presentation was between the creative element and the marketing element. (Note: 50/50 would rate a "10").
9. Between 1-10, rate how well you think you'd get along with the agency people.
10. Between 1-10, rate how sincere you think the agency will be toward caring about your business and how well it will balance your interests with those of its other clients.

Once you have completed all of the agency presentations, compare your rating system sheets. If two are close, then talk about the strengths and differences with the other reviewer(s). Decide which agency you want.

Then call the agency manager and tell them you want to work with them. At the same time, set up a meeting to iron out how they will be paid. (Covered in an upcoming chapter).

Out of courtesy, call the other participating agencies to let them know and also thank them for their proposals in a letter. If, by chance, the chosen agency doesn't work out, you can go back and consider one of the others.

You don't have to follow this Agency Selection

Guideline exactly. It can be formed comfortably around your own business methods.

Another point. It doesn't matter if an agency is a 4-A (American Association of Advertising Agencies) or has any other rating or affiliation. What matters is how they'll work for you and whether they will produce results.

There is no perfect way to pick an advertising agency. But this method is better than eenie-meenie-minie-moe.

> *If managers of creative people could only understand what time means and how important it is to the creative process. The quality of the product is directly related to the amount of time that goes into it.*
> — *John M. Keil*

Chapter Seven

Setting the Ground Rules with Your Advertising Agency

Staying on the front burner with solid agency management

Whether you're looking for a consulting firm or full scale advertising agency, the following principles apply to both. To make it easy, I'll just refer to agencies.

Before you listen to any agency proposals, here's fair warning. I know the way the advertising agency selling machine works. In fact, I almost decided to remove myself from the business altogether because of it.

You see, an aggressive, healthy agency needs clients. So, it's oriented to get new business. When the agency pitches the client, everything . . . from the proposals to its people . . . is meant to woo you. It's meant to be impressive. And usually it is.

But the problem with a lot of agencies is that once

Setting the Ground Rules

you're in the boat, a lot of that impressiveness disappears. Why? Well, largely because the agency is after another new account and you, for the most part, are put in a maintenance mode. You are assigned a different account executive and creative team. Some people call it being back-burnered.

And that's the part I don't care for. You hired an agency in the first place to get the best advertising you can . . . and then the main energy of the agency is directed at acquiring new clients, not toward your account (and all their other accounts, for that matter).

The biggest problem is that most businesses don't know the difference. And if they suspect something is wrong, they don't know what to do about it.

Before I went into the advertising agency business, I decided that I'd only take on clients if I could fully handle their advertising needs . . . even the needs they didn't know about. Then I could work with a company with a clear conscience and know that I was doing all that was possible to make their business better.

There are other agencies that have that attitude, too. You can recognize them in many ways.

1. They don't pitch every opportunity that comes up. In fact, they are quite selective toward the clients they would like to do business with.
2. They gladly provide client lists.
3. Their clients are satisfied because their advertising is working.
4. The agency's clients have been with them for a number of years.
5. The same people that worked on the initial proposal also work with you on a continuing basis.

My advice is to look at the advertising agencies that want to work with you and see if most of these items match.

But no matter how an advertising agency appears, it's always possible you might get back-burnered anyway. However, there's a sure-fire way to avoid it.

It's called advertising agency management. And it's something you simply *have* to do when you work with an advertising agency. You have to remember that you are the boss.

The main contact with your agency is your account executive. The A.E. is the one who helps you develop what you should do and executes the projects through the agency creative and media people.

First of all, you have to like your account executive. You should trust him. You should respect his judgment. You should be able to communicate with him easily. You should consider his opinions and abilities an asset to your advertising. You should feel that he really cares about your business.

If you like him, but he agrees with you on everything you say, you don't have a good account executive. You have a very expensive tape recorder.

Developing a good relationship with your account executive is the first step to good advertising agency management. Once you have that kind of relationship, you not only will be able to communicate your ideas well to him, but he should be able to *anticipate* your needs and come up with solutions you never thought of.

If you *don't* like your account executive, ask your agency for a different person. If that doesn't solve the problem, look for another agency.

Next, sit down and develop a budget and project schedule you both can live with. I prefer a six-month schedule that's revised every three months. Discuss how often you should have regular meetings. *Then stick to your schedule.*

If your agency starts missing the deadlines you both created, you're probably being back-burnered. Don't allow it. Tell your A.E. that you are unhappy and want to get back on your original plan.

If that doesn't work, call one of the agency principles and explain your concerns. Don't worry about the problems you might cause your A.E. A good agency would like to know if one of its A.E.'s is not doing his job.

Time is important. If you aren't satisfied with the solutions offered within two weeks time, then begin to look for another agency immediately.

You cannot afford to have an agency that can't stick to the schedule they developed with you. Your business is simply too important.

If your advertising isn't producing anticipated results or the agency is constantly going over budget or they aren't providing you with the service agreed to, I would try to correct the situation in the same manner.

There are good advertising agencies in this world. There are also bad ones. The smart businessperson should know that it could take several attempts to find the advertising agency that will work for him.

Don't be dismayed if the first agency you hired didn't live up to your expectations. Just cut the line as soon as you can and begin fishing again. Once you find the right agency, your business may benefit tremendously.

Setting the Ground Rules

If you manage your agency properly, you'll get the full benefit of its talent, knowledge and skill. If you don't, some other client will.

The only things worth learning are the things you learn after you know it all.
— **Harry S. Truman**

Chapter Eight

How to Pay Your Advertising Agency

After you've gone through the exhausting procedure of choosing someone to help you with your advertising, the last thing you probably want to do is talk money in detail.

Most common: "Well, I really don't know *what* or *how* they're going to charge me, but I'll reserve judgment until after their first bill. If it's within reason, everything will be okay."

I don't know why people take such a soft approach when they initially hire an agency. Perhaps it has something to do with handing over the "trust" of taking care of one's advertising. They may associate the "trust" of handling their advertising with the "trust" of the subsequent billings that will occur. Well, I'm no psychologist. I just know that it's not common sense to just "wait for the bill."

I'm sure some agencies don't mind. After all, this way

they've almost got carte blanche.

This will probably be the most read chapter in this book. Businesses will love it. And the reason is quite simple. I know of no other guide published anywhere that says what I'm about to say . . .

Compensation to advertising agencies is negotiable. In fact, more often than not, it's the client that determines how the agency is paid for its services.

Trouble is, since the client doesn't know anything about the advertising agency business, it's hard to negotiate. So they usually adopt what the agency proposes in the first place.

You want to pay a fair price for good service. And only you and your agency can decide what those figures are. There is, however, a balance to be achieved. After all, you don't want to pay more than necessary. But you also don't want to pay too little and get a shabby advertising product.

First, let's examine what an advertising agency is. It's a business that spreads the cost of its overhead (building, employees, etc.) proportionately over a number of different clients.

Often its high-priced marketing and creative talent would be too expensive to hire for just one business. But by getting its clients to share the costs, the agency can provide a superior advertising product for them.

Okay, now you basically know *why* you have to pay an agency. The question is how?

Let's understand one thing. When we talk about paying an agency, we're not talking about production costs. We're talking about paying for services . . . like art, marketing, research, copy, creative direction, etc. You'll be charged separately for out-of-house charges like type, color separations, radio and television production, etc.

Basically, there are four ways to compensate an agency.

1. Percentage of media budget.
2. By the hour.
3. Monthly retainer.
4. Cost plus.

Each has its advantages and disadvantages. Some businesses mix and match features they like from each. The following information should provide you with the essential tools to make a good determination.

Percentage of media budget

This used to be the most traditional way of paying for an advertising agency. In fact, agencies used to say that their services didn't really cost anything because the 15% media commission would pay for the copy, media analysis and order placing services.

However, it's really not a very good system. Why? Because it's not based on the work, it's based on the buy. For instance, if you had a $15 million media budget, $2.25 million dollars would probably be too much to pay your agency. If your budget was only $75,000, compensating your agency $11,250 might not be enough.

Let's pretend your agency prepares a new campaign for you and you hate it. They've already "spent" the amount the budget provided, but they have to do it over.

The agency looks at this situation as a loss. Even if

they come up with an alternative campaign you like, you can bet it will be developed on a "spend as little time and money as possible" basis.

And that's not what good advertising is all about.

Or what happens when the budget is cut mid-year and much of the creative is already developed? The agency has already spent the money it expected to receive. Unless the agency is compensated on an extra basis in this case, bad feelings usually arise. And that's not good fodder for advertising, either.

Also, many clients don't like the 15% media basis because they believe their agency might overstate the media budget in order to get more money. And they might be right. What I've found is that agencies that work on this basis utilize commissionable media a lot more often. And they use media such as billboards more often because it pays a larger commission rate. That's seldom in the clients' best interest.

The 15% method applies to commissionable media but not well to many things advertising agencies do for their clients today, i.e., brochures, P.O.P. displays, sales films, exhibit design, etc. These are things agencies can do for you that have no commissionable basis at all. And they can't be expected to do them for free.

An agency that works on this basis also usually marks up all out-of-house expenses by 15-25%. So you are really paying a lot more for production, typesetting, etc., as well.

Some agencies bill out long distance telephone calls that they make on their clients' behalf. They often even charge their clients for the office supplies they use . . .

even for the copies they make.

Can you imagine charging your clients for the paper clips you used? Brother!

So, as you can see, I don't believe the 15% method is a very equitable way of paying for advertising for the agency or the client. There are better methods that are a lot more fair and easier to keep track of.

Methods that eliminate being billed for your share of the agency's copy machine.

By the hour

This is one of the simplest methods to pay for an agency and one of the best if you do not anticipate a long term relationship or want to establish a trial basis. It also gives you a good idea of what things cost in the real world.

Whether monthly or by project, the agency simply lists the time spent by the agency members who participated. You'll pay a certain amount an hour for your account executive, the copywriter, the creative director, the artist, the media buyer and whoever else played a role in developing the advertising.

It's as simple as that. If you want it done over, they'll do it over. And charge you for it, of course.

In this manner, you get a good cost accounting of the work that went into the project and the agency is fairly compensated for the work performed. You'll be able to analyze your actual expenditures for the different facets of the advertising process. If you're considering doing some of the work in-house, you'll have a good idea if it's economically feasible. (Of course, if you do some of the services in-house, you'd pay your agency less because it would be doing less.)

"By-the-hour" also works on projects that might not have a commission basis.

You'll still have to ask whether or not the agency marks up its out-of-house expenses. Remember, it's a negotiable item.

Another negotiable item is the media commission. Although the most common procedure is to let it pay for the copy, media analysis and media buying, you can negotiate alternatives. It can be rebated to the client in full. It can be applied toward the fees billed on the hourly basis. Or perhaps your agency would rather get the commissions and charge you a lower hourly rate. There is no "right" way to do it. It's up to you. Keep in mind though that you'll be charged for traditional services that media commission normally pays for if you choose an alternative method.

Paying your agency by the hour is a good, tangible way of keeping track of what it costs to create your advertising. If you are going to have a long term relationship with your client, the next two methods may be even better.

Monthly retainer

For continuing, long-term relationships between the client and the advertising agency, the monthly retainer method is usually the most fair for both parties.

Normally, the fee is based upon the average number of hours of services the client would use during the course of an average month. Sometimes it also includes a share of the agency's cost of doing business. So it's not much different than the hourly-basis method.

It evens out your expenses for advertising services over the year. The theory is that an agency might do half the work one month and twice as much the next, but the retainer is the same.

I think this is a much more mature method because it looks at each partner in the advertising relationship as a businessperson.

Retainers can offer some real advantages. First, once the retainer fee is negotiated, you can budget the expense over the course of the year, eliminating surprises. You know what the expense will be.

In addition to the financial terms of the retainer, the length of the agreement should also be discussed. For example, if you set the terms of the agreement for one year, you are ensuring that the agency will have the time and talent to meet your advertising requirements *when you need them to*. It's like buying a box seat at a baseball stadium. The seat is there for you to use, anytime you want.

On the other hand, there are some real advantages for the agency, too. First, since the agency has a guaranteed steady income, it can forecast its own course better. By relying on a certain amount of work for the course of the contract, it makes it a lot easier to plan for the future — how many employees they can afford, etc.

Second, since the retainer is steady income, the agency is less likely to be going after every other account that comes up.

So the retainer agreement creates a relationship that truly benefits both parties. If needs grow and the workload increases beyond expectations, there should be a provision in the contract to renegotiate the retainer prior to expiration. You should also provide an easy way to get out of the contract for yourself just in case you change your mind about the agency.

Again, remember that the retaining fee is negotiable. There is no right or wrong. There is nothing you *have* to include or exclude. It's all up to you and your agency.

Just like the hourly basis, the commissions and out-of-house expense mark-up are negotiable as well. Although your agency might squirm a bit when you bring up these points, it's best to get everything out, discussed and agreed upon at the very beginning.

Cost plus

As with retainer agreements, cost plus accounts are billed on a monthly basis and the terms are usually specified by contract as well. The difference is the way the compensation is figured.

The agency bills the client for a portion of all out-of-house expenses, overhead, salaries, office supplies, etc., plus a mutually agreed upon amount for profit. Normally, an agency will mark-up its expenses by 17.65% of net. Why 17.65%? By the laws of mathematics, it's a way to figure out the traditional 15% fee basis. Try it. Multiply a figure by 17.65% and add it together. Then subtract 15% from the new total. You should end up with the same original figure.

Media commissions are usually applied toward covering a portion of the monthly expense if you use a cost plus method.

No matter what method you choose, remember that the purpose is to pay a fair price for top quality advertising, not to simply cut down on the profits of your agency.

Choose the system you think is the best and cover all the points before you begin work with the agency. If everyone agrees on the basis of the advertising services expense up front, you are going to have a very healthy agency relationship. And that is one of the best ways to create great advertising.

One last thing. If you really want to make your agency run for the money, do what a lot of companies do with their top sales people. On top of your compensation agreement, include a bonus based upon reaching your sales objectives.

If, for example, your budget is $750,000 for the year, you could offer a 1.5% incentive if your sales goals are met. You'd be amazed how hard your agency will work and the extra paces they will go through to make sure you reach that goal.

After all, isn't that what this whole thing is about?

The world of advertising is highly enclosed, neurotic, self-reverential — a jungle where drumbeat and grapevine and bright plumage and chest pounding count for a lot, where protective coloration is for losers.
— *James Kaplan*

Chapter Nine

Keeping Your Agency on the Right Track
Evaluation and Review on a Regular Basis

Most businesses hope their good employees will stay around and not look for new jobs. They provide other benefits beyond salary to keep them there. After all, hiring a new employee is both an expensive and time-consuming process. Replacing an employee who's far along your firm's learning curve is difficult because it takes someone new a long time to really "get up to speed."

What's this got to do with your agency? Plenty. Some firms use the simplest excuse to drop their agency and look for another one. In fact, I know companies that have actually used half the agencies in my city.

And I believe an agency is as important to a company as an employee. Staying with an agency can provide a much stronger consistency to your advertising program over the course of several years. Eventually, they may know just as much about your firm as you do. Maybe more.

Your agency will develop a learning curve that should be an asset to your firm. It's something that shouldn't be disregarded easily.

So what can be done to keep you from firing your agency when things go wrong? What can you do to keep your agency from leaving you for greener pastures?

The answer is simple. Try to avoid problems in the first place. Good advertising agency management is the answer, again.

This time it takes the form of an on-going agency review program. On a regular basis, say every six months, you should sit down with your advertising agency and go over the agency's performance over the last half of the year . . . and decide what can be done to improve.

Some great advertising agencies in this world already incorporate such a program in their course of business with their clients. They know a client in the hand is worth two in the pitch anytime.

By using the following form, you can "grade" your agency on an on-going basis. It's also helpful for your account executive to fill out the form as well.

Once the forms are complete, go over your answers and see how they compare. I've found the enhanced communication is amazing. More times than once, I've discovered that the client perceived strengths where I thought I was weaker, and vice-versa.

It's also a good idea to pull out the forms you did six months ago and see if there has been improvement over that period of time.

Keeping Your Agency on the Right Track

Such an exercise gives you a tangible reference of how your agency is performing . . . and it also establishes a guideline for the next six month period.

The form I use looks something like this:

AGENCY EVALUATION REPORT

Agency Name: _____
Client: _____
Name: _____
Position: _____
Date: _____

The following Evaluation Report was created to help rate the performance of your agency's work on an ongoing basis in an objective manner. It is a tool for better communication and correction, if necessary.

Please check your answer
in the appropriate box, with
5 being the highest on the scale.

I. AGENCY PERFORMANCE

A. Marketing

	5	4	3	2	1
General Knowledge of Company					
Product Expertise					
Creating Strategies					
Executing Plans					

B. Creative

Development of Ideas					
Execution of Plans					
Ideas & Creative Ability					
Timeliness & Scheduling					
Production Ability					

C. Media

	5	4	3	2	1
Media Knowledge of Market					
Good Representative Contacts					
Getting Proper Authorization					
Budget Control					

D. Others (Please List)

Keeping Your Agency on the Right Track

II. PERSONAL PERFORMANCE OF ACCOUNT EXECUTIVE

- Creative & Imaginative
- Gets things done
- Able to communicate
- Keeps costs efficient
- On time & reliable
- Dedicated to Company
- Gets along with staff
- Cooperative level
- Handles things professionally

III. WEAKNESSES AND STRENGTHS

_____
_____
_____
_____

IV. IMPROVEMENT SUGGESTIONS

_____
_____
_____
_____

By using a form like this, you can keep your agency on course and working the way you want it to work for you. It also helps your agency keep track of your changing needs.

It's difficult to take the time out of a busy day and do a six-month agency review. We all believe the immediate takes precedence over what happened in the past or what could happen in the future.

But if you're serious about having . . . and keeping . . . a good advertising agency, then force yourself to complete an agency review exercise on an on-going basis.

Your long-term advertising goals will benefit because of it.

There's a bigger fool than the fellow who knows it all; it's the fellow who will argue with him.
— **Garth Henrichs**

Chapter Ten

How to Work With Your Account Executive

"Instructions on how to work with my account executive? Why do I need instructions? I work with different business people every day and I get along just fine."

There's a difference between "getting along" with people and "getting work" out of people. If you've ever employed people, you know the difference.

For some reason though, a lot of business people want to make their account executive their pal instead of their working partner in business. And then all the disciplines it takes to do good advertising seem to go right in the wastebasket.

After all, it's hard to tell a friend that the work is lousy. And it's hard for the A.E. to tell his "friend" that the idea he just came up with is a real stinker.

So, my advice is, at least at first, conduct the business between you and your account executive in a strictly professional manner.

Now, I'm not saying that friendships can't or shouldn't develop. Some of my best friendships happen to also be my clients. The difference is that those friendships happened after working together for a long period of time. And I think the foundation of any relationship based upon honesty, mutual respect and trust can lead to a good friendship.

If you do develop friendships with your account executive, just make sure the relationship is open enough to welcome criticism on both ends. And never, never let a friendship with your account executive stand in the way of an important business decision. If the agency is bad and the account executive is the nicest guy in the world, switch agencies.

There are two things to think about when you work with your account executive.

One, your A.E. has other clients. So it's unfair to expect unrealistic deadlines or personal attention at your beck and call. Response in a normal businesslike period of time is appropriate.

Two, your A.E. is responsible for handling your account. That means that between the two of you, meeting times, work schedules, presentations, etc., should be hammered out on a mutually satisfactory basis. If you don't effectively plan your account executive's time with you accordingly, some other smart client will take up the slack.

I suggest a standard meeting time, once or twice a week, to cover the basics of the advertising schedule.

How to Work with Your Account Executive

During this time you can discuss your plans, approve presentations and keep track of your schedules. Some businesses prefer a flexible schedule. At any rate, make sure that you make the time to let the account executive do the job he or she was hired to do. If you don't, you're simply not getting your money's worth.

The other major thing to watch out for in your account executive relationship is scapegoating. The larger the agency, the easier it is to scapegoat . . . that is, blame someone else or another department for something that's gone wrong.

Let me give you an example:

Your account executive delivers a proof for a magazine ad and he wants you to approve it. For the sake of example, a lot of things went wrong with this ad. The explanation goes something like this:

"I need you to approve this ad right away because its got to be in New York this afternoon. Now the photograph isn't exactly the way we talked about because the photographer insisted on shooting the scene with pineapples in it. Our copywriter got a little crazy with the words, but I think it will work. The media buyer didn't buy your space in time so we didn't get the position you wanted . . . but at least it'll be in the right issue. And since the production department was in a hurry, here's a black and white version of your color ad. Write your signature here on this approval form, okay?"

Can this nightmare happen to you? It's possible.

Most businesses would yell and scream under their breath at the scapegoats and tell their A.E. to send the ad. Wrong.

Your account executive *is* responsible for directing your advertising. There *never* should be rush problems unless you initiated them. You should *never* settle for photography, art or anything else that you didn't approve of or don't care for. You should *never* approve something you can't see, such as not being able to see the color with a black and white proof. And, by the way, who's paying for all the rush charges?

It's not the scapegoats' fault. It's your account executive's fault. Problems happen, sure. But your A.E. should be seasoned enough to plan things in advance so problems can be corrected before you see them.

Chances are he forgot to tell the media buyer about the ad until it was almost too late. He didn't tell the creative director *not* to use pineapples in the ad and was too busy to help oversee the shooting. And the production department didn't know it was a color ad until yesterday, thus the black and white proof.

That's a horse of a different color, isn't it?

Chances are, you'll never have a disaster like I just mentioned. But be on the lookout for the scapegoat when you work with your account executive.

When a scapegoat does appear, explain to your account executive that you feel he's responsible for the work or schedules he delivers to you. If he doesn't feel good about them, he should take corrective measures before you see them. Tell him you don't believe in scapegoats.

Being an account executive is a tough job. It carries a lot of responsibility.

But if you pay an agency for its services, you pay for an account executive that does his or her job.

A good A.E. can make good advertising seem easy to do. A poor one can make even mediocre advertising a wrestling match.

Remember, set working guidelines with your account executive that you'll be happy with.

And don't let the scapegoats interfere with your advertising.

Real seriousness in regard to writing is one of the two absolute necessities. The other, unfortunately, is talent.
— Ernest Hemingway

The point of good writing is knowing when to stop.
— L. M. Montgomery

Chapter Eleven

How to Work with a Writer

Since I'm a writer by trade, this chapter is especially dear to my heart.

Writers in the advertising business are usually called copywriters. This is not to be confused with copyrighters, who I suppose are lawyer types that specialize in copyright protection of ideas, books, etc.

Before we get into *how* to work with a writer, let's look at *why* you even need someone to write for you in the first place. After all, we all learned how to write in school, right? What's the big deal?

For some bizarre reason, a lot of people who would never tackle art in a million years think they can write as well as anybody. But if I remember right, we studied art in school, too, didn't we? Why aren't those people "Art Pros" as well?

I think it's because we all do some sort of writing

everyday. Memos. Letters. Little notes on the refrigerator. So it seems natural to believe that almost anyone can write a brochure or an ad if they know something about the subject.

That's where some people step off the diving board. Because it's simply not true.

The subject matter *is* important. But what's more important is the ability to *communicate* with a designated audience. And that's what a good writer or copywriter can do.

Most people struggle with just getting the facts on the paper. A writer takes those facts and refines, simplifies, condenses, colors and orchestrates the words that contain those facts. Then he or she composes something that's *interesting* to read. And frankly, that's the main difference.

When you're paying $4000 for magazine advertising space . . . or newspaper space . . . or television time . . . doesn't it make sense to do whatever you can to ensure that people will pay attention to it?

People who recognize their own writing limitations aren't just smart. They're usually rich, too.

When a client says to me, "I've written down most of the facts I'd like to see in this ad, but I can't put it together. Do you think you can write it?" I smile. Because that person finally understands what writers are for.

So, let a good writer tackle your advertising copy. The small amount of money you spend on the writer will pay for itself again and again in results.

You see, a copywriter does more than just write copy. He's also an idea and concept person. In fact, a copywriter will often provide a "copywriter's rough layout" that indicates how he visualizes the advertising he wrote for.

Now, if you're working with an advertising agency, there's a good chance there's a copywriter or two on staff. If your agency *doesn't* have a copywriter on staff, look for another agency.

And don't let your agency substitute its account executive as your writer. The worst advertising I've ever seen was written by the A.E. for his client. It was no better than if the client wrote it. He should have read the first part of this chapter.

If you're not working with an advertising agency, you can still get great writing help by hiring a freelance writer. These independent souls have usually worked with an advertising agency for a number of years and have decided to start their own copywriting business. They usually know what they're doing, because that's how they make their living.

Freelance writers usually work by the hour. So you can compare different writers by weighing their hourly rate against the time it takes them to complete a project. Remember though, a $60 an hour writer who completes your job in six hours is essentially the same as a $40 writer who takes nine hours to finish the work.

The best way to compare any writer, freelance or not, is by the actual work that they do. Ask to see it. If you like the writer's style, then that's the person for you. If you are unsure, see some more writers first before you make a decision. As strange as it seems, the saying "I don't know anything about writing, but I know what I like" applies in this case.

Also, a word about awards. If a writer receives a lot of advertising awards, it *is* a good indication that he/she is a good writer. Maybe great.

But awards are usually given on the basis of creativity, not results. So ask the writer what kind of results occurred with those award winners. If the writer is knowledgeable about the success of his work, you've got a writer who cares about making you money. And that can be as good as gold.

So, you've realized you need a writer and you've found a good one to use. What's next?

Establishing a working relationship, of course.

First, establish the goal. Tell the writer you want to create a brochure on your new line of European furniture.

Second, define the assignment. It's one of the most important things you can do. Tell the writer that it's for a four-page brochure and if you can, explain the audience that it will be reaching. For example, "we're trying to reach yuppies" requires a different writing approach than "we're trying to reach high income men and women who are interested in antiques."

Third, give the writer as many facts as you can about the project. Competitive brochures, details about the subject matter, trade articles about European furniture, *anything that could help* the writer understand the world that he's writing in. Write down what you'd like to see in the project and discuss it with the writer in detail.

If you can furnish a rough layout of the brochure from the artist, the writer can judge the copy area and write to fit. I recommend this very strongly.

Fourth, let the writer ask questions. You'll probably

get a lot of weird ones, but answer them anyway. Many good writers can redefine the assignment and make it better after they understand what the project is about. I play "devil's advocate" at this stage of the game because it's a fast way to find out how clear all the project elements really are. I've redirected the main thrust of the project many times by just asking a lot of questions.

Fifth, determine an hourly estimate of the project. "How many hours do you think this will take?" is a very legitimate question that usually can be discussed right at the beginning. If an appropriate amount of hours can be agreed upon between you and the writer at this point, you're not likely to get a "surprise bill" later on.

Sixth, determine a deadline. For your needs, you should create a deadline that will allow time for major copy changes and revisions before your ad has to go into production. Naturally, we hope the copy doesn't need major changes, but planning a buffer in your schedule is a good idea, just in case.

For the writer's needs, you should establish a schedule he or she can live with. The writer probably has other work besides yours and it all has to be arranged in a schedule, too. The client who frequently fails to allow enough time for good work will either lose a good writer or get shabby work.

Seventh, make sure to give the writer the telephone numbers required to be able to ask more questions. Many times I'll run into a question in the middle of writing and I'll come to a dead stop until that question is answered. By allowing adequate access to you and other sources, you can avoid many writing delays.

Finally, let writers do their job in their own way. The

more structure you give them, the less creativity you'll get in return. Let *them* put the elements together first. And then take a look at how they did it. You'll probably be pleasantly surprised.

Remember, you're using the writer because you liked his style. Let him use it on your project.

Once you get the finished copy back, read it over thoroughly before saying anything. It's easy to stop in the middle and say "you left out *this!*", but then you might feel foolish when you discover it's on the next page, where it should be.

Once you've read the piece, ask the writer why it was put together the way it was. You'll get a much better understanding of the work the writer put into your project.

If you have major problems with the work, talk to the writer about it now, not later. Discuss the problems you have and create a new plan to rewrite the project and solve those problems.

Most of the time though, you won't have problems with the work. Professional writers have an ability to comprehend what needs to be done and to create the approach required. A few word changes here and there and you've got yourself an *interesting* presentation of your copy. Copy that people will read. (Or see and hear in the case of broadcasting work).

And if you want the same writer to do great work for you on a continual basis, a few "attaboys" won't hurt. (Change it appropriately for woman writers, please). Most writers pour their guts out in order to write good copy . . . and it's nice to know when it's appreciated.

If you want your advertising to work the very best it can, put the writing into the hands of a professional. At the cost of media nowdays, it's essential that you squeeze out as much success as you can.

Unless you're Ernest Hemingway, a writer probably will do a better job than you would. And in case you didn't know, ol' Ernest started out as an advertising copywriter.

A capacity for childlike wonder, carried into adult life, typifies the creative person.
— **Kaiser News**

> *The creative person is unique in that during the initial stages he prefers the chaotic and disorderly and tends to reject what already has been systemized.*
> — *Ralph J. Hallman*
>   *Journal of Humanistic Psychology*

Chapter Twelve

How to Work with an Artist

Sometimes I think advertising agencies were invented so businessmen wouldn't have to work with artists.

That's a bit of an exaggeration, but there's truth in it. Because artists aren't the easiest people to work with, even if you do it every day.

At first glance, you might think this chapter is only for people who hire freelance artists. But it's for everybody. Even if you work with an advertising agency, there still may come a time when you and the agency artist will interact.

First, choose an artist like you choose a writer. Carefully examine the artist's previous work. Ask how much he or she charges an hour. Get a cost estimate on the pending project. Then pick the right person or persons for the job. Unlike writers, it may be a good idea to use more than one artist per project, especially if one is good at illustration and one is good at graphic layout and design. Just because the person is an artist doesn't automatically mean he's good at everything. In fact, it's a good idea to ask the artist what he likes to do. Chances are, it'll be his specialty.

Normally you don't run into problems of "rights" when you work with a copywriter. But when you work with artists and photographers, you often do. So it's a good idea to spell out who gets what before you even begin.

For example, let's say you commissioned some nice illustrations for a brochure a year ago and you'd like to use them for this year's Annual Report. You call up the artist for the originals and she says, "I'll have them there tomorrow, but I'll need to pick up a 'use fee' check of $750.00 and the originals will have to be returned in two weeks; after all they're mine."

You say, "Whoa, I paid you to do those last year!" She says, "No, you paid me a one time use fee for those illustrations." And so it goes.

Get the message? There's no reason why you should have had to pay for using them a second time . . . but if you didn't *write down* the terms of the agreement when the job was initiated, you're in a gray area. And that means trouble.

So, before you begin the project, spell out the terms. Fully describe what you want done, set the deadline dates and note who has the "rights" for the work. Then get the artist to sign it. "Rights" are negotiable and a lot of artists like to retain them.

I hire a lot of artists to do work. And at least ninety

percent of the time, I retain all the rights.

Working *with* the artist is another matter. There is no finer example of the creative persona than an artist. But since many of the same characteristics apply to other talents, too, let's talk about creative people in general for a moment.

Creative people are normally quite independent. They often have little interest in things like company politics and don't put a lot of value in job security.

They don't enjoy routine-type work. They're resourceful and persistent. Skeptical and critical. Assertive and precise.

Often, creative people are just as easy to get stimulated and prolific as they are to get irritable and nonproductive. They can be stubborn, compulsive and emotional. And you probably wouldn't want them around at all unless it was for their spirit of adventure, originality and spontaneity. But those are the ingredients that make good advertising.

Creatives are complicated people. They can be tough to communicate with. But their innate ability to develop something out of thin air outweighs any difficulty and makes the struggle of working together always worthwhile.

I enjoy the artistic mind. The way it works fascinates me. And if you *can* communicate what you want to do, you'll normally get a lot better job than you bargained for. Here are a few tips to get the best work possible out of artists:

First, tell the artist *what* you want to accomplish with your project. Take a few moments and explain the problems you're trying to solve and the audience you're trying to reach.

Second, tell the artist *why* you chose his or her style or ability . . . and *why* it's important to the feel and look of the project. Point out things in the artist's portfolio that you like.

Third, discuss style. If you are looking for the artist to do something a certain way, get some examples to show. The artist isn't a mind reader.

Fourth, let the artist come up with the visual solutions. Answer all the questions, but don't dictate specifics. And set a date to see the ideas in rough form.

Fifth, try to imagine what the artist's final art will look like when you see the rough sketches and ideas. If you can develop this ability, it'll save you money. It gets quite expensive to completely do up an idea visually and then abandon it. During the rough sketch stage, let the artist know if he's on the right track.

If you see something you don't like, don't say, "this is terrible, I hate it" . . . even if that's how you feel. You'll lose your artist's enthusiasm. Say something like, "I was thinking of a bolder approach here" or "Eels are a little strong, maybe a school of goldfish would work better with the copy."

I repeat, let your artist come up with the visual solutions. Your job is to lead the horse to water . . . and give it time enough to drink.

Sixth, talk to your artist as a professional. If you're uncomfortable about an idea he has, explore the thought process of his mind. Treat him as an expert and you'll get expert results.

Seventh, go over the final production art carefully and make sure it represents your discussions during the rough sketch stages. You'll probably have a few adjustments to make here and there . . . and the time to make those adjustments is during that meeting, not later.

Finally, go over the corrections and make sure everything is perfect. Then, thank the artist for all his input and work. The positive re-enforcement will pay dividends the next time you work together.

When it comes to artists . . . or many other types of creative people, remember the old saying, "You can catch more flies with honey than vinegar."

As long as it's sincere honey, of course.

The essence of the creative act is to see the familiar as strange.
— *Kaiser News*

A photographer is able to capture a moment that people can't always see.
— **Harry Callahan**

The intellect has little to do on the road to discovery. There comes a leap in consciousness, call it intuition or what you will, and the solution comes to you and you don't know why.
— **Albert Einstein**

Chapter Thirteen

How to Work with a Photographer

Precautions to take before you see what develops.

Whether you use an advertising agency or not, you are more likely to work with a photographer than with an artist or writer. So this chapter is important, too.

First of all, if you're thinking about taking those pictures you need for your brochure yourself, think again. Professional photography can't be matched by just anyone who "has a nice camera." Don't believe that you or a friend can take photographs "just as good and a lot less expensive" than a pro. Unless you're a real exception, you can't. And you'll pay for your poor photography many times over in lost results.

Like artists and writers, photographers are also a special breed of person. In order to be good, they have to be part-artist and part-technician. And they have to have an ability to interpret what you would like to see into images you can use.

Just like artists, you can choose photographers by looking at their work and deciding which one is best for your project. Some specialize in people, others in architecture. Some are better color photographers, while others do their best work in black and white.

Photographers work on either an hourly basis or a project basis. For short term projects, I recommend an hourly wage, with an upfront estimate of how many hours it will take. For long term or larger projects, you can often get a better deal by contracting the job for a set fee.

The biggest mistake people make when using photographers is not defining the project clearly enough. Write down the parameters of the project and how you're going to use the work. Tell the photographer if the work will be used in black and white, color, or both. That'll tell him what types of film he'll be shooting.

Also include all shooting times, deadline information, film charges, developing costs and most important, *who* owns the negatives and transparencies after the work is done.

There are a lot of books, articles and guides to this subject alone . . . and the subject of ownership has gotten considerable attention during the last few years. Most courts have upheld the photographer's rights to ownership of film he shot unless different ownership terms were agreed upon and defined.

In other words, unless you deal with the subject of ownership right at the beginning of the job, you more than likely are paying for photographs for one-time only.

And the next time you need them, you'll pay the going rate for using them again.

The important thing to remember, though, is that you *can* own the photography and prevent ongoing charges. It's just a matter of negotiation. Some photographers simply won't do it. Some will charge an extra fee. Others, who would like to work with you on a continual basis, will let you have all the work after the project is finished and consign all rights to you. The latter is the most advantageous.

Of course, you can see the benefit of the photographer owning the work. Not only could he resell portions of it to you as each need occurred, he could also resell it to anybody else. Unfortunately, I'm not in business to benefit photographers. So, if at all possible, I negotiate all rights to the work prior to the project.

A good trick is to get hold of one of those "I have to have the rights" photographer contracts and use the same language for your contract ownership instead. Chances are that contract carries the most up-to-date legal terms available.

If you're shooting pictures that'll never be used for color, use black and white. If you're shooting applications you'll need in both black and white and color, have the photographer use both black and white and color film.

But if you're primarily shooting color and maybe will need a few black and white shots later, consider shooting color only and making black and white versions of the work when the needs arise. Even though you may sacrifice some quality, color to black and white conversion technology has become quite good. You'll save a bundle from shooting the same thing twice with different film.

You can always get black and white from a color negative or transparency. But getting color from a black and white negative is impossible, unless you color it by hand or with computer techniques.

Speaking of film, I recommend shooting color transparencies for most color applications. First of all, transparencies can be directly used in most color separations that are used for printing. Negatives have to be made into prints or transparencies before they are separated. And the more times an image is processed, the more it deteriorates the integrity and quality of the image.

Second, with transparencies, what you see is what you get. With prints, you don't know if the negative was bad or the color of the print was bad. Or both.

Third, you don't have to worry about the photographer keeping, losing or messing up the negatives because there aren't any with transparencies. Transparencies are the originals.

Fourth, when I do need a black and white print, I have an internegative made of the shot that I want and the results are normally quite satisfactory.

Fifth, you can immediately find the photographers who have a negative attitude. Use the ones who have a transparency attitude instead.

Without getting into a lot of technical mumbo jumbo, here's another thing to remember. The larger the image area of the negative or transparency, the greater your flexibility of use. So, for most professional applications, I prefer using a 2¼" square format over a much smaller 35mm format. In some cases I even use a 4" x 5" format.

Why? Let me put it this way. Even if you use the same

ASA speed of film in all three film formats, an 8 x 10 enlargement of the 35mm version will be grainier and less distinct than an 8 x 10 enlargement using the 2¼" or the 4" x 5". You also have greater cropping flexibility. A 2¼" transparency can be cropped by over half the image area and still be larger than a full frame 35mm format.

It always happens. You save a little money by hiring a photographer with a 35mm to take a few, small shots for a brochure. They turn out fine. Then the boss likes them so much, he wants a big 30 x 40 print for a poster. Oh oh. The 30 x 40 enlargement looks like a picture made with colored salt and pepper. You should have used a bigger film format.

Sometimes for action shots, portability or speed, 35mm is still necessary. But my advice is to use at least a 2¼" image area whenever possible. And use low speed film, 100 ASA or less whenever you can. There's nothing more disappointing than taking a fantastic photo on 400 ASA and seeing the grain pop up when you create an enlargement.

Another professional trick to remember is to make sure your photographer "brackets" his shots. This is done by taking the shot with the correct f-stop, then purposely underexposing and overexposing the same shot by one or two f-stops each.

Why would you purposely waste such shots? Remember, film is a lot less expensive than getting the photographer back to the location (and models, products, etc.) to reshoot the shot. So, bracketing is insurance in case the light metering is misread . . . or developing turns sour. If your photographer was an f-stop off, you don't have to settle for a shot that's too dark or too light. You've got a perfect one instead.

I once worked with a company photographer who would never bracket his shots. He thought it was "unprofessional." We took more retakes than you can imagine and settled for way too many dark and light shots. If I could have hired another photographer, I would have.

That same photographer also reminds me of another important thing to remember. Always double-check how much and what kind of film your photographer takes to a location. I once had an important shot to cover that would take place at 10:00 A.M. at a satellite plant. Although I had talked to the photographer about the shot and what I was going to use it for the day before, just before we left I asked him, "Got enough film?" "Yep," he said.

We got there in time to set up and have a few minutes to spare. "How many color rolls did you bring?" I asked. "Color?" he questioned. "I just brought black and white." Umph. There was no time to get more film. So we used what we had. I had a lot of explaining to do, later.

I learned to never take common sense for granted when it comes to a photographer. I always make sure the photographer takes all the types of film I need or may need and I always have him bring a lot more film than I think I'll use. It's a lot better having it on hand when you need it than wishing you had brought it.

Make a point to check on the film before going to the shoot and you'll save a few gray hairs for your older years.

Finally, for your own protection, make sure the

How to Work with a Photographer

photographer's model release is good enough to meet your legal needs and make sure you or your photographer get a signed release for any model you use.

Here is an example of what a Model Release should contain. Please check the laws in your state to make sure it applies to all the aspects you need it to cover.

SIMPLIFIED ADULT MODEL RELEASE

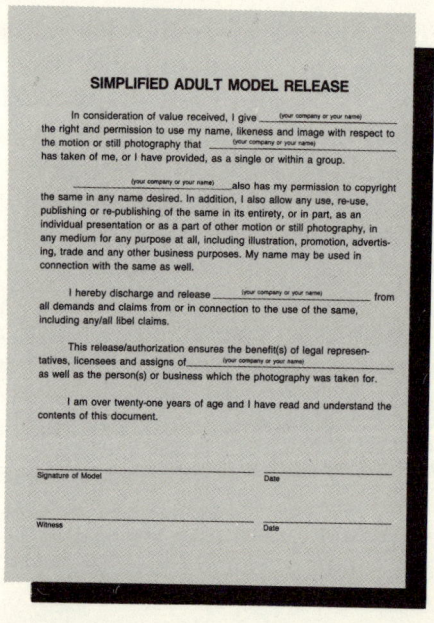

In consideration of value received, I give _____ (your company or your name) the right and permission to use my name, likeness and image with respect to the motion or still photography that _____ (your company or your name) has taken of me, or I have provided, as a single or within a group.

_____ (your company or your name) also has my permission to copyright the same in any name desired. In addition, I also allow any use, re-use, publishing or re-publishing of the same in its entirety, or in part, as an individual presentation or as a part of other motion or still photography, in any medium for any purpose at all, including illustration, promotion, advertising, trade and any other business purposes. My name may be used in connection with the same as well.

I hereby discharge and release _____ (your company or your name) from all demands and claims from or in connection to the use of the same, including any/all libel claims.

This release/authorization ensures the benefit(s) of legal representatives, licensees and assigns of_____ (your company or your name) as well as the person(s) or business which the photography was taken for.

I am over twenty-one years of age and I have read and understand the contents of this document.

Signature of Model _____ Date _____

Witness _____ Date _____

Photographers are normally pretty easy to work with. They work with more different types of people than almost any other creative group.

Just define the project and determine the terms up front. And don't be afraid to ask to see the shot yourself through the lens. After all, you're paying for that privilege.

> *People do not come home from work at night to watch anybody's advertising.*
> — Roy Grace

> *The higher advertising involvement goes in an organization the better the advertising.*
> — John E. O'Toole
>   Chairman
>   Foote, Cone & Belding

Chapter Fourteen

Why Media Planning and Buying is so Important

Creating your advertising is only half the job. The second half is buying your media properly so that it does what it was designed to do.

Most full service agencies offer "media buying" as part of their complete advertising services. Other businesses called "Media Buying Services" will plan and implement your media buy. These services normally receive the same 15% commission on media as agencies do and will work for that fee or less.

Media buying is a lot more complicated than you might think and I recommend using one of these two services rather than doing it yourself.

But that doesn't mean you shouldn't understand media buying basics. After all, how can you evaluate a media plan properly if you don't know what you're looking for?

And that's what this chapter is about . . . the fundamentals of buying media. We'll cover more specific areas when we deal with the individual advertising media in upcoming chapters.

Good media plans are almost a science. They hit the right people the right number of times at a cost you can afford. But often the major mistakes made in media planning are not the media planner's fault.

Three common problems can occur when a business owner sits down with a media planner. I hope you can avoid these problems.

The first is the *egomaniac syndrome*. He'll buy media he doesn't need because he either thinks it's prestigious or wants to see his advertisement on a show or newspaper or magazine because it's one of his personal favorites . . . no matter who the audience is. The conversation goes something like this: "I like your preliminary plan, but there's no TV in it that I watch. I like Jeremy's Whale. It's on at eight on Channel 3. Let's put our commercials on that instead." "But, but . . ." stammers the media buyer.

The second thing that can occur is the *greed syndrome*. This guy will purchase anything that's a good buy, even if it really won't do his media buying any favors. "I heard that the new weekly newspaper is offering 2 for 1 ads *and* a *FREE* dinner for two if we just buy their package. Let's do it!" "But," says the media planner, "it's not a good buy for the audience we want to reach." "Yes," the owner smiles, "but no one else is offering a free dinner, either."

That reminds me of the old joke that told of the man who lost one of his contacts in the living room but looked for it in the kitchen instead. The light was better.

The third I call the *unspecific syndrome*. The media

planner wants to know the audience he should design the plan for and asks, "who should we be selling to?" The owner replies, "Just about everybody, really. I can't think of a person in America who shouldn't buy my product." That poor media planner has his job cut out for him. What the owner *should* have said is: "Our creative is targeted at young adults, say 20 to 45 in age, with annual incomes of $40,000 or more. Yuppies, you know." At least then the media planner *could* have done his job.

So, defining your demographics . . . the people you want to specifically reach . . . is the first and most important thing you should do before you begin any sort of media planning or buying.

Once that is done, there are more things the media planner has to think about. How well does each commercial spot or ad *reach* your demographics . . . and how many times does your demographic see or hear your message?

Reach is a very important media buying concept. It's defined as the *total audience an advertising medium actually covers*. With different research and rating materials, the media buyer can determine what media is the most efficient to use to satisfy your demographic goals. For example, if adults, ages 20-45 *are* your main demographic, the beautiful music station you listen to may not be the best vehicle to reach them. But a contemporary station might be.

And your media buyer can figure out the most efficient cost by comparing the cost of the buy with comparable alternatives. For example, if a 30-second spot costs $40 and reaches 8,000 people in your demographic, how does it compare to a 30-second spot on another station that only costs $20 but reaches 2,000 of the people within your demographic?

A media buyer would use a "cost per thousand" evaluation and tell you that the cost per M (M means 1,000) for the first station would be $5, versus the second station's $10 per M spot cost. The $40 spot is much more efficient.

After buying a good "Reach," the second thing a media buyer worries about is Frequency . . . that is, how many times does your audience see or hear your message.

Even though advertising is not a science, there are a few things we do know. And one of those things is simply that your message is absorbed better if a person sees or hears your advertisement more than once.

Advertising people generally agree that a good media plan should reflect a schedule that hits as close to 100% of your demographic as possible, with a frequency of 5 to 7 times. That is the formula you should always strive for. It is a good indicator of whether or not you're spending too much or too little on media.

If an adult in the 20-45 age group sees or hears your message six times, your media buying was successful.

A more complicated formula, called Gross Rating Points, is used by media buyers too, usually for television. Gross Rating Points, or GRPs, are actually a total of all the *rating points* of each specific program you bought for commercial time. *Rating points* are defined by an audience survey, often conducted by the American Research Bureau (ARB).

If 200 households reported watching a certain program out of the 1,000 interviewed in the survey, that program would be given 20 rating points.

Media Planning and Buying

For instance, five spots on a television show that reaches 20% of the households creates a formula like this: 20 × 5 = 100 GRP's. (Ratings × Frequency = GRPs). But what about demographics? ARB surveys and others that provide ratings usually list a breakdown of audience demographics of the programs they rate.

So if you want to reach women between the ages of 18 and 35, you would want to locate the programs that attracted the best share of that demographic first, then figure your GRPs. Rating points alone should never be used as your only criteria.

Media buying is a complicated business and you shouldn't have to do it yourself. Find a media buyer who you have confidence in and take the time to let him explain all the systems, like some I just mentioned, that make your media buy a good buy.

These formulas are designed for advertising campaigns that utilize more than one facility within the advertising medium . . . and they work even better when you advertise on several advertising media at once.

There is a term you should be familiar with called Synergistic advertising. It just means that advertising on different media using the *same message* at the same time is more powerful than advertising on the same advertising media at different times. The collective advertising effect of Synergistic advertising is greater than adding up the ratings of each medium separately.

So, if you advertise your product on radio *and* newspaper, your advertising effectiveness should have a greater impact than buying the same number of GRP's on radio or newspaper alone.

The idea behind this theory goes something like this:

If I hear a commercial on the radio and hear it frequently, I'll remember that spot. But if I hear the spot on the radio, then see the same message in the newspaper, I'll remember it sooner and maybe better, because my mind has received that message in two different ways.

Naturally, this applies to more than radio and newspaper. It could be TV and radio, billboard and newspaper, direct mail and TV, or three or four (or more) advertising media working together at the same time, supporting the same message.

A good media planner and buyer will "weave" synergistic advertising into your media plan. And it should have an even stronger effect than the GRP's indicate.

Media buyers also do something else that is advantageous. They negotiate costs.

Most advertising media supply a standard rate card when you want to buy some time or space. If you're Mr. Average, you'll pay the going rate.

However, media buyers buy time and space for clients all the time. And that gives them leverage and a better understanding of what you should be paying. To make a long story short, they usually can get you a better deal than the one on the standard rate card. Sometimes a lot better. A good buyer can save you hundreds and thousands of dollars with successful negotiation. It's another good reason to use a media buyer instead of trying to do it yourself.

I've seen a lot of businesses that truly believe they are saving money by setting up their own pseudo advertising agency for the purposes of getting the 15% advertising commission. The 15% is chicken feed in comparison to the efficiency and effectiveness that a qualified media buyer can bring to your advertising campaign, not to mention the money you'll save on negotiated rates.

Very few in-house advertising agencies buy enough media to create as successful a plan as a media buyer.

Remember: Define your demographics, use the most efficient media, make sure the reach and frequency work together properly and utilize a synergistic campaign whenever possible.

And let your media buyer do the work he's paid to do.

I like print because it's "user-friendly." Print was interactive before we invented the term. Television is great, but it talks at you. And for all its appeal, it's still a fairly inflexible medium. You turn it on and you can watch this channel or another channel. But you can't move ahead to midnight or the next day or move back in time to this morning. You can't tear out a piece of a program and hand it to a friend.
— **Keith Reinhard**
  Chairman
  Needham Harper Worldwide, Inc.

Chapter Fifteen

How to Buy Print Advertising

Print advertising is one of the elders of the advertising world. It dates back to the discovery of the written word.

Even though print's relatively new broadcasting brothers sometimes seem more exciting and alive, nothing beats print for the things it is especially good at.

Someone once said that the word content of an entire evening's television newscast took about the same amount of words as ¾ of a newspaper's front page.

Print is excellent for detail. It's good for selling a lot of items. If you miss something when you read an ad, you can read it again. You can't instantly replay a radio or TV commercial. And it's a good medium to mention price. Prices can be circled in the newspaper. And compared. But in broadcasting, prices, along with phone numbers, can go in one ear and out the other.

You can also offer coupons in print. That can be another advantage over the other media.

To buy print advertising you can either go through your advertising agency or get it directly from the newspaper or magazine sales representative.

The advantage of buying it through your advertising agency is that the agency will take care of all the details and you usually don't have to pay for the buying effort. The 15% agency commission takes care of that.

However, a lot of local newspapers don't give agencies a commission. Why? Because they have their own *sales team* and believe a commission to both the agency *and* to their salesman is redundant.

I've never quite seen the logic of all this, since it *is* the agency that delivers your ad, copy ready, to the newspaper's front door. Where does a salesperson enter into it? There are sales people in broadcasting and other advertising industries, yet they somehow compensate the agency 15% for the business it brings in.

The reason I mention this is simple. If your newspaper does business the way I just described, make sure your advertising agency understands that you *will* pay for their media buying when the newspaper won't. If they don't understand that, they just might subconsciously "help" you select alternative media that does grant them a commission. That's a fact of life.

Although I've never seen a study on this, it wouldn't surprise me if at least 20-30% of all radio buys could and should have been newspaper buys . . . if there had been a commission to the agency. Maybe someday the newspapers will wise up.

Okay, so a lot of newspapers have their own sales team. They assign a salesperson to your business and that person becomes your "personal representative." Even though these people are often salaried employees, they usually are also paid a small commission and often have their own pocketbook at heart rather than your best welfare.

They aren't the best people to ask things like "how large should my ad be?" or "how often should I run it?" or "do you really think advertising in this special section will do me any good?" Questions like that make dollar signs light up in their eyes.

One of their favorite lines is ". . . you don't have to *pay* for an advertising agency to make the ad for you . . . we'll do it for free!" Ever hear the saying "you get what you pay for?" Remember it.

You can open up your newspaper and spot the ads the advertising agencies have done. They look different. They stand out. You stop and read them. The ones that all sort of look the same are the ones the newspaper did for free. You can't blame the newspaper. The ads they produce are just assembly-line products.

But the purpose of advertising in print is not to just be in the newspaper. The purpose is for the readers to read it. And that's why I suggest that you should *never* let the newspaper make up your ad. Let your agency do it. Let a freelancer do it. Make sure your ad is one of the different ones and you've got a chance that it'll work for you.

Now, figuring out how big your ad should be and how many times you should run it is not an easy process. There's no set formula to follow because it depends on *what* you're selling, *how many* items you want to mention, and *how long* the sale will run. It also depends on the type of image you want to create for your business. (See chapter on Positioning).

I said you shouldn't talk to your newspaper advertising representative about it because that's a little like asking the fox to watch the hen house. But who do you talk to? Your advertising agency, of course. They know you and your business and the media you'll be using, too.

But if you don't have an advertising agency and want to do it yourself, just use plain old common sense.

It's foolish for me to try to describe a scenario because your business and product has to be tailored to every different advertising situation. But here are a few tips:

1. When you want to reach different advertising demographic segments, consider using different ads and place them where each demographic will see them. (i.e. rings — Women's section, men's watches — business section). If you try to sell to too many different demographics in one ad, it won't end up attracting anybody's attention because it doesn't initially interest them.

2. Make sure your ad gets in the section that is most logical for that readership. Put entertainment ads in the entertainment page. Put fishing and hunting ads in the sports section. Don't be clever and think that your ad will "stand out" if it's in the wrong place. Chances are it'll just be overlooked.

3. Talk to the audience you want to reach in the ad headline. Shoppers. Hunters. Joggers. Whatever. *Looking for a Boat but Can't Float a Loan?* is more powerful than *Boat Loans Available.*

4. Figure out your reach and frequency. Try to achieve a 5-7 frequency during your sales period and size the ads to the dollars you can afford. A good idea is to initially do a large ad and support it with smaller ads to bring up the frequency. People who buy full-page ads often break the frequency rule by buying less than 5-7 times. But those advertisers usually use the newspaper a lot during the course of the year.

5. Use synergistic advertising if at all possible. Support your newspaper advertising with other media such as radio, television, billboards, transit or direct mail.

The best advice I can give you on print ads is this. Go through the newspaper or magazine and cut out the ads you like . . . the ones that attracted your attention. Study them and ask yourself why. Maybe it's their design. Or the way they were written. If you can figure out what you like about them, circle the best features and give them to your artist as an example of the type of ad you want to create.

Stand out with your advertising. Be bold. Be different. For fun, take an interesting test tomorrow morning. *After* you've read the morning paper, get a pad and write down the ads that you remember. Unless you're thinking about ads when you go through your normal routine, I guarantee you it'll be a short list.

Create an ad with the look that would capture *your* attention when *you* read the newspaper and you'll discover that the ad will probably attract attention from other people, too.

Don't be afraid to repeat your ad, either. Chances are

that you'll get sick of it a lot quicker than your readership will. A print ad is good for at least three showings, no matter what.

We've talked about newspaper a lot in this chapter because it's certainly the most common print advertising application. Magazines are also an interesting form of advertising that can be used to address a more specific demographic. For instance, if you buy *Good Housekeeping* you get a lot different readership than if you buy an ad in *Playboy*.

What a lot of people don't know is that many "national" publications have programs to run local ads in local areas. In many places you can advertise in magazines like *TV Guide*, *Newsweek* and others and buy only a city or region or statewide circulation. The best place to ask about your area is . . . you guessed it . . . your advertising agency.

Most of the same advice I give about newspapers applies to magazines, too. I wouldn't let them create your ad, either. For a monthly publication, I'd figure 5-7 times a year would be adequate frequency.

If you are considering advertising in a magazine, buy several issues of it and read it. If you are still seriously thinking about advertising in it, call the sales representative of the magazine and ask for an "Ad Kit" (don't worry, it's almost always free). It'll supply you with all the information you'll need to know, including rates, special stories that might pertain to your business in upcoming issues, etc. See if there are any special sections that your product would benefit being close to. See if you have any competitive advertising in the magazine and think about how you can advertise better than he does.

The more complicated your message . . . the more

detail you want to present . . . the more likely that print advertising is the best medium for you to select.

Print advertising can be done very successfully. And it can be done very badly. But newspapers and magazines just wouldn't be around if they didn't make money for *most* of their advertisers.

As in all advertising, I recommend getting professional advice. Make ads that stand out from your competition and all the other ads that surround it. And *please* don't forget to sell when you've got the reader's attention.

The average network news telecast contains as many words as one-half on the New York Times front page.
— *Media Messages*

Some people will believe anything if you whisper it to them.
— **Louis B. Nizer**
   Thinking on Your Feet

TV just feeds you. Radio involves you.
— **Himan Brown**

Radio is a creative theater of the mind.
— **"Wolfman Jack" Smith.**

Chapter Sixteen

How to Buy Effective Radio

Advertising on radio and other types of broadcasting media is different than print because your commercial disappears after it's played. While print advertising can be savored, radio advertising is consumed.

If a commercial plays at 7:20 in the morning, you just can't listen to it again if you missed the address or phone number. You have to wait until the commercial plays again. That's the nature of broadcast advertising.

Now while all this may seem rather obvious, understanding this difference plays an important role in *how* you buy radio time. Frequency is a vital element in radio's effectiveness.

Since you can't automatically recall the radio commercial and hear it again, you've got to hear the same commercial two, four or six times before the message sinks in. If you missed the address the first time, you consciously or subconsciously are hoping the commercial will return soon so you can get the information you need. That's the way radio advertising works.

And that's also the way you should buy it.

Most of the time, radio should be bought in chunks. High frequency over a short period of time is much more effective than low frequency over a longer period of time.

Why? So your audience can hear your spot again and get more information out of it.

For example, if you wanted to advertise a two-week campaign and you could afford 42 radio commercials, I'd recommend the following buy:

Tuesdays, Wednesdays and Thursdays, 3 spots between 7-9 a.m. and 4 spots between 3-6 p.m. for two weeks. Notice that I concentrated both my day periods and my hour periods.

This utilizes something I call the *Radio Splash* theory. By advertising in concentrated areas in tight day groups, you seem larger than you really are. And believe it or not, people hear your concentrated campaign for two or three days and they think you're on all the time.

Now the amateur might buy three spots every day on the station for 14 days. That's 42 spots as well. But the campaign would not be nearly as effective.

Think of the *Radio Splash Theory* like throwing rocks in a pond. A handful of large rocks makes a bigger splash than throwing a tiny pebble a bunch of times. And it attracts more attention.

Buying radio time poorly was probably *not* the poor amateur's fault. He was probably sold the time by an overzealous radio salesperson.

You see, radio time is priced differently at different times of the day. The most expensive time is called drive time, which is normally 6 a.m. to 10 a.m. and 3 p.m. to

7 p.m. It's called drive time for a simple reason. It's when people are driving to and from work. And it's also the time when people listen to their radios. So listenership is usually higher during those periods than any other time.

Late morning, early afternoon, evening and late evening rates are lower because fewer people listen. But it leaves the radio station with a problem. How can they sell all that time that isn't prime?

Well, the "good ol' boys" in radio came up with something called T.A.P., which stands for *Total Audience Plan*. T.A.P. normally splits your buy into thirds, giving you ⅓ drive time, ⅓ late morning/early afternoon and ⅓ evening. "Total Audience" is a bit of a misnomer because you're attempting to hit the station's entire audience, even when there are just a few listeners. Who really cares if you buy 100% of the station's audience?

What's really important is buying time when people are listening, not when they're not. And T.A.P. buys you only ⅓ of the most desirable time.

But T.A.P. costs less and it's attractive to a lot of "shoppers" . . . like the radio-buying amateur I mentioned earlier. Unless there's a darn good reason (and there are a few), you should *only advertise when people are listening*. And that means buying drive time, even if it costs a bit more.

Think about this for a second. The people who understand *how* to buy radio (usually advertising agencies) buy up the most effective times. That leaves a lot of time the station wants to sell. So by selling T.A.P.'s and other promotions, they effectively sell their station's available airtime . . . and it's usually sold direct to businesses that don't know much about the nature of radio.

When you talk directly to a radio representative, you take the chance of being talked into some special deal that includes the airtimes the professionals don't want. But if they don't want those times, you shouldn't either.

I'd break the *"Radio Splash Theory"* under a couple of conditions.

For instance, if I signed up sponsoring a popular show on a daily basis, say something like the *Paul Harvey Show*, I'd be only advertising once a day . . . but the audience is much more regular. Within a week, there's a good chance they'd hear my spot at least 3-4 times.

Also, I have bought commercials in late morning/early afternoon, evening *and* T.A.P., but only for specific audience or timing reasons. If your audience is housewives, you might be better off advertising in late morning or early afternoon. Or, if you have a 24-hour restaurant, evening or late-evening commercial time could remind the people to come in during those late hours.

Personally, I've found T.A.P. to be most effective in the summer when people are listening to the radio more hours in the day. Events that appeal to mass popularity, like concerts, circuses, fairs, sports, etc., seem to be the best suited for the nature of the T.A.P.

That brings up an interesting medium phenomenon. Radio listenership increases in the spring and summer, while the audience for television increases in the fall and winter and decreases in the summer. This is an important consideration when you are picking advertising media to use.

Of course, it would be ideal to advertise on the station you listen to and that's all. But it might not be good advertising.

A good radio campaign should use, if possible, three or more stations with spots scheduled at the same time. That's because it often takes at least several stations to get a demographic reach similar to other media like television or newspapers.

You may have 20 or 30 radio stations that share your market. But most cities have one or two newspapers and four or five television stations (not including cable). Using several stations to achieve the same demographic share is simply common sense.

To find the most popular stations in the demographic(s) you want to reach, it's important to look at the most recent surveys. Your advertising agency can supply them or you can usually ask any radio salesperson for a copy.

Arbitron, often referred to as the "A.R.B." or "Arb," is one of the main publishers of radio surveys. These surveys tell 1.) How many people are listening during certain times of day on each station in your market and 2.) A demographic breakdown of those listeners.

If you want to advertise to teenage women, just see what stations are most popular in the corresponding demographic segment. The surveys usually tell you the best time to reach those teenage women as well.

The world revolves around supply and demand. So, expect to pay top dollar for the most popular station in the market. When a survey comes out, radio stations revise their rates accordingly. In fact, most stations have "price levels" in their rate cards so they don't have to go to the print shop every time they change rates. They just change levels instead.

But since we're talking about costs, also remember this: Radio may be the most negotiable advertising medium in the world. One of the reasons is that there *are* a lot of stations in every market and competition for your advertising is keen.

It doesn't matter if you or your advertising agency does the negotiating, either.

You'll get the best results when you plan your advertising purchases ahead. If you're planning to advertise a week a month for three months, ask the radio station for a package deal. Get comparisons from similarly-rated stations. You should be able to get price reductions, free commercial times and free participation in special promotions by committing your dollars in a schedule you probably were going to buy anyway.

If you make a major radio buy, you should *never* have to pay a standard rate card price.

I like radio because you can buy both demographics and audience. You can reach a certain *number* of people and a certain *type* of people. If you're selling a rural product, like western bootwear, it's not hard to pick the music format of the station you'll advertise on. Business products work well on All News stations. And the beat goes on.

Radio delivers exclusive types of audiences. In some cases you don't get nearly the number of people, but you get a highly *targeted* group of people. And the more precisely you can hit the audience you're trying to reach, the less you pay for reaching *Waste Demographics* . . . or in other words, people who are not in the market for your product or service.

But buying efficient airtime should not be your final goal. Getting the audience to *listen to your commercial* is the only way you're going to influence their behavior and sell them.

Ever notice how a lot of the commercials on radio sound the same. Guess what? They were probably produced by the radio station, using the same announcers and the same old tired, assemblyline techniques.

My advice is just the same as it is for print advertising. Be different. Be bold. Stand out from the crowd. And don't let the radio station write and produce your spot. Nine times out of ten, you'll get the kind of commercial that people ignore or turn down instead of up. And all the trouble you went to to get the right audience and the right stations at the right price will simply be wasted.

I suggest using your advertising agency or a good audio commercial production house. If you use these services, make sure they don't pass off an ordinary spot on you and let the station produce it anyway. Make sure there's a spark that could ignite your audience's attention. And make sure you don't use the same announcer who works on the station that you're buying time on. Again, don't forget to sell.

A few tips:

1. If you're including your address in the commercial, simplify it. Instead of "134525 East Pines," say "at the corner of First & Pines, next to Gumbies." It's easier to remember.

2. I hate phone numbers in radio because I just can't imagine people remembering them or writing them down. If you have to mention your phone, refer to the yellow pages in the phone book. If you aren't in the phone book, put an ad in the newspaper and mention that instead.

3. Radio does work better when you combine it with other advertising media. Remember the synergistic approach? You can even cheat a little by mentioning your newspaper ad, TV commercial or billboard inside your radio commercial.

4. Check out the price differences between 60-second commercials and 30-second commercials. Normally, 30-second commercials are only ⅓ less than 60s. And that makes 60-second commercials a lot better value.

Remember. Radio means repetition. Use the *Radio Splash Theory* and make your advertising seem more extensive than it really is. Radio is a versatile and quickly changeable advertising medium that can work very well for the common business. As long as you use common sense, that is.

> Picasso once said, "Taste is the enemy of creativity." Even good taste imposes a limitation on creativity, leading to a formalized, academic, lifeless and predictable art.
> — Roy Grace

> They say 90 percent of TV is junk. But 90 percent of *everything* is junk.
> — Gene Roddenberry
>   TV producer

Chapter Seventeen

The Lure of Television

Making sure your Investment Pays Off

So you want to advertise on television, eh? After all, it is the most influential advertising medium . . . and you know most people watch it.

And since you talked to that TV sales representative, you now know that it wasn't as expensive as you thought. Why, the guys at the station will even put together a commercial for you for three or four hundred bucks.

Hold it. Hold it right there. Hold on to your wallet and your enthusiasm for a minute and read this chapter before you proceed any further.

Television advertising may not be for you.

Plain and simple, it costs more money than most other media. When you advertise in print, you can fit the size of your ad to the dollars in your budget. But when you advertise on television, it's difficult to cut costs without cutting your reach or effectiveness.

Television is expensive for two basic reasons: Its Area of Dominant Influence (referred to as an A.D.I.) and the cost of good commercial production.

In most cases, the television signal reaches far beyond what most radio stations can. A lot of smaller towns have their own radio stations but receive their major television programming from larger adjacent cities. A television station often exceeds the reach of newspapers in the area, too.

That's what A.D.I. is all about. Most of the time, television is king of the A.D.I. because it reaches more people than any other media. For example, a television station might be seen in half the state, whereas the same area has six major newspapers and 256 radio stations.

Unfortunately, part of the expense of television is that you pay for reaching all those people. So in reality, the cost of advertising time on television is relative to other media in comparison to the number of people it reaches. You are spending the same amount of advertising dollars if you pay $1,000 a commercial to reach 500,000 people on television or pay $100 per radio commercial on 10 stations that reach 50,000 people each. Or in other words, each purchase is equal to a cost of $2 a thousand.

But one of the biggest mistakes most advertisers make when they use television is that they really didn't need to reach all those people. They really only needed to reach a 25-mile radius of their city and they ended up paying for a 100-mile radius. That translates into wasting a lot of advertising on people who will never respond. It also means that 25-mile radius could have been addressed more efficiently by advertising in another medium.

Television isn't expensive to businesses that can fully take advantage of the station's A.D.I. and sell to all the people their commercial message reaches.

But if you can't take advantage of the majority of the audience you're paying for, it's a good signal to look at alternate ways of spending your media dollars. However, a lot of advertisers ignore this type of advice and spend a lot more money than they should.

There is something magic about being on television. If people see a product on TV, it somehow has instant validity. The advertising claim "Seen on TV" is done for a good reason. It works.

Cable advertising is an interesting alternative to the A.D.I. dilemma I just illustrated. With cable, you can still advertise on television, but only to where the cable goes. And sometimes that's the only area you want to reach anyhow.

The disadvantage to cable is that you usually can't advertise on the major networks. You *can* advertise on various sports, music and news channels, though. And if they attract the demographic profile you want to reach, cable advertising can be a very good advertising buy. Since this medium is still relatively in its infancy, the cost per spot is normally *much* lower than standard broadcast time.

But no matter *what* you pay for advertising time, you still need to fill that space with an influential pitch that will sell your product or service.

The second aspect to the expense of television advertising is commercial production, that is, making a TV commercial. *Effective commercials cost money.* There are no bargain basement deals.

It's important to understand why you need a good commercial. Unless your commercial is seen and heard, it is worthless. You must capture your audience's attention in the midst of some strong competition. And what's your competition? A run to the kitchen for a quick snack. Discussions and conversations between the program. Channel switchers who want to see what else is on. And worst of all, the dreaded flush factor. (Known politely as bathroom visits).

Your commercial has to be interesting enough to keep your audience from doing all these things when it appears on the screen. Then it has to sell.

Sound like a tall order? It is. And that's why television commercials are expensive. It takes good writing, production, direction and creativity to stand out from all the rest of the commercial garbage that people have learned to tune out. I honestly believe that 75 to 80 percent of all television advertising is *so mediocre* it's ineffective.

If you choose to advertise on TV, invest in a commercial that *will* be effective. You'll then take full advantage of the power of that medium.

Who should produce your TV commercial? Normally not your television station. In my own mind, it's the equivalent of letting the newspaper ad department create your advertising.

TV commercial production is another reason advertising agencies exist. They've got the writers, directors and other creative people to do the job. Look at the agencies "reel" (a collection of the commercials they've made) and see if you like their style. If you do, discuss a budget and let them do it.

You can also hire a production company to do your commercial, too. In most cases they have the talent available to deliver the same sort of product. Just like the agency, ask to see their reel and discuss your commercial budget up front.

And while we're on the subject of television commercial budgets, get ready for a shocker. The average cost for a 30-second national commercial now costs between $75,000 to $150,000 on up to produce. A regional spot costs between $35,000 to $60,000 on up and a local spot can run between $5,000 to $20,000 on up.

Production costs are going up all the time. If you have really good creative people working on your project, they sometimes can come up with a concept that fits all the criteria but is simpler than average . . . and achievable with a smaller budget. That is the only way I recommend trimming TV commercial costs. If you trim quality, you're trimming the chances of success.

With the advent of cable and video players, more people are watching more of some sort of television than ever before. Because of the sheer quantity of programming, the television audience, in general, has become more sophisticated.

You can no longer get away with the type of shoddy commercial production that sold thousands of Veg-a-matics.

Want to hear another epitaph? "If I'm paying this much for a commercial, I want to be on it myself. That way everyone will know who I am." I've seen so many bad commercials made with the owner or daughter of the owner and not with professional talent I wonder why they still appear. Yet they do. Ego wins, commercial loses.

The Lure of Television

Don't get me wrong. Television is perhaps the most effective of all advertising media. Your audience can see and hear your message at the same time and that utilization of two senses improves your odds for influencing their behavior.

But it isn't minor league advertising. It should be used only if it doesn't dramatically overreach the audience you intend to sell to. You have to be able to afford a television schedule that meets the standard requirements of reach and frequency. And you have to budget enough money to create a commercial that will get your audience's attention.

Those are all factors that should be considered before you ever spend a dime on TV. If you don't have a product or service that justifies the amount of money you'll have to spend, consider using one of the other advertising media instead.

Good television advertising can produce significant results. Just make sure it makes sense for you to use the medium and make sure you're ready for the investment to do it right.

Television is a medium. They call it that because a lot of stuff you see on it is neither rare or well done.
— ***Bits & Pieces***

Everything should be made as simple as possible, but not simpler.
— *Albert Einstein*

The great art in writing advertisements is to find out a proper method to catch the reader's eye.
— *Addison*
  The Tatler

Chapter Eighteen
Advertising on Billboards, Buses and Benches

Keep it simple and synergistic

There are other ways to advertise besides using electronic or print media. One of them is called Outdoor Advertising.

Some people equate Outdoor Advertising with just billboards, but I prefer to think of it as the advertising you see outdoors. Billboards, posters, advertising on buses/trains (called transit advertising) and even park benches.

This is an interesting category because this is advertising that makes up a portion of the environment we live and work in. You are exposed to it whether you want to be or not. You can't avoid it by changing the channel or turning the page. In a way, Outdoor Advertising truly has a captive audience.

However, the nature of the medium also limits its use.

It is a "glance" type of medium. Even if it's great advertising, it still can only steal a second or two of a person's time. People will not stop their cars and read a 30-second message on a billboard. Nor will they run along side of a bus as it travels through the city to read a lengthy message.

Outdoor advertising is useful if you want to make a single, simple statement. That's why it is normally used as a secondary advertising medium in a synergistic campaign. It's an image enhancer and a good message reminder. But it's not a workable medium for any kind of detail.

Your message usually has a lot of frequency in Outdoor Advertising, largely because you buy it by the week or month, rather than days or seconds. That gives people who are exposed to your message a lot of different opportunities to see it. That makes Outdoor Advertising very appealing for some messages. You have to remember, however, that it probably also has the greatest "tune-out" factor. Once it's seen once or twice, the message can easily be ignored.

Now here's a gospel rule to follow when creating your Outdoor Advertising: *Use no more than 5 to 7 words in your advertising message.* It's hard to restrict what you want to say in such a short message. But if you want it to work, do it.

You've got to remember that 95% of the time, either the message or the audience is in motion. And in order for your message to be effective, it has to be read all the way through in a single glance. Your graphics or pictures should be basic and uncomplicated . . . and easy to see from a distance.

The simpler the message, the more effective it will be. Creativity is important, too, because *how* the message looks and *what* the message says have a lot to do with getting your audience's attention for that brief period. It also has a lot to do with your message being remembered.

For most cases, Outdoor Advertising should not be used as a solitary medium. Its greatest effectiveness is achieved when it's coupled with a radio, TV or newspaper campaign . . . and then only to re-inforce the basic campaign themes.

Plan your production carefully and intelligently. After all, creating a painted billboard or 60 transit panels is not a cheap process. If you can make them general enough in nature to use them as theme lines for several different campaigns, you'll save a lot of money.

Outdoor Advertising is not a good medium to use for a short, week-long campaign. But if your campaign stretches over a month or two, it can be an excellent reminder between the times you're actually advertising on the other media.

Buying the right location is just as important as buying the right time on radio or TV. If you can't get the right high traffic location for your billboard, or you can't buy several billboards closely surrounding your business, don't buy. If your business is downtown and you can't buy space on downtown area buses, *don't buy*.

As with other media, Outdoor has a lot of unpopular inventory that the salesperson has to sell. Often a salesperson will try to "tie-in" a few bad buys with a good buy. And although you can't blame him, you certainly don't want to buy poor locations.

Billboards, Buses and Benches

My advice is to negotiate the best deal. If you get some poor locations for free, it's better than nothing. But if you end up paying for poor location, you have no one to blame but yourself.

Don't ignore the power of Outdoor Advertising. Used properly in a synergistic campaign, it can really perform well for its cost.

But please, don't forget the 5-to-7 word rule. Even if your advertising agency breaks it, consider shortening it anyway. Don't take a chance of not being read at a glance.

In the jungle of the market place, the intelligent buyer must be alert to every commercial sound, to every snapping of a selling twig, to every rustle that may signal the uprising arm holding the knife pointed toward the jugular vein.
— Dexter Masters
  The Intelligent Buyer and the Telltale Seller

> *The sign brings in customers.*
> — *La Fountaine*

Chapter Nineteen

Signs—the Other Outdoor Advertising Medium

Signs are probably the oldest advertising medium in the world. But you'd be surprised how little most advertising executives know about them.

That's because, for the most part, signs are not a commissionable medium. An A.E. might say, "If you can't make money off them, why know anything about 'em? Just get something to let people know where you are and we'll spend the real advertising dollars somewhere else."

This is one subject that I suggest you *do not* discuss with your advertising agency. Many account executives will attempt to talk you out of any significant sign expense because they think they see "media dollars" they could have flying out the window.

I've always found this ironical, because good signage is essential to most successful businesses. And unsuccessful businesses can't pay agency bills. So it would make sense to me to consider signage a priority. Some

Signs

may, but most don't.

In fact, a lot of times, the cost of signage doesn't come out of the advertising budget at all. It should, though. Because it *is* a legitimate advertising expense.

If your business depends upon people locating and going into your establishment, signage should be important to you. And if you have a high traffic location, *it's essential.*

A high-traffic location is an important consideration to many businesses. In fact, most of the time you pay a premium for it. But why? Simple. All those people who travel by every day are prospective customers.

So your sign becomes more than just an identifier to that traffic. It performs the same job a billboard does by creating frequent impressions in your prospect's mind. Frequency, as you remember, is a very important advertising element.

Your sign does a lot more than simply tell people where you are. It *advertises* your location and your business to all the traffic that goes by . . . and that can account for a lot of people.

Let's say 5,000 cars go by your place on the average every day. Using a factor of 1.9 people per car, 9,500 people have actually been exposed to your sign. And that's just in one day!

Here's another important thing to consider. When you advertise in a city-wide advertising medium (like radio or newspaper) there'll be a lot of people across town who won't respond simply because your business isn't *convenient*. A good majority of your customers live or work in close proximity to your business.

That means a sign is an efficient advertising medium

because it advertises to people who are most likely to respond. *People traveling by your location.*

I call this *Neighborhood Advertising,* since the people who live, travel or work within your business' neighborhood are affected and influenced by your signage.

Neighborhood Advertising is one of the least expensive and most effective forms of advertising a business can do. Consequently, it makes sense to do it right.

The first thing to remember about signs is to keep them simple. They should be readable from a good distance away. That means 0-3 words and your basic logo. And if your logo is too complicated, simplify it.

Since I don't recommend your advertising agency to help you solve this problem, who can you consult for creativity? Good question. By using your own common sense and a freelance artist/designer, you should be able to rough out the type of sign you'd like.

Take that rough sketch to a sign company and find out if it is feasible (they will check for city ordinances, etc., that can restrict sign use) and give you an estimate of cost.

However, knowing *what kind* of sign you want can help you determine *what kind* of sign company to talk to. You should choose a sign that is right for both your type of business and location. If you don't really know what that is, check out what similar businesses have done in other nearby cities. You'll get a bunch of good ideas.

There are several types of good signs. The least expensive sign is the painted wood sign. In some applications, it's all that's necessary. Look up "Signs" in the yellow pages and visit at least three sign painters to survey their work and gather ideas and estimates, including the cost of installation. Make your decision and order the sign.

Instead of a painted sign, you might consider an embossed, or carved wood sign. These are more expensive because of the process it takes to make them. They are more decorative and are most effective when an artist flair can enhance your image and where "walking" type traffic is predominant. I'd pursue this type of sign in the same manner.

The most common sign today is the plastic sign and plastic letter sign. They've become the industry standard because of the versatility of plastic material. They can be colored in thousands of colors and molded in many shapes. Such signs can be back-lighted or front-lighted. And the lightweight strength and durability of plastic gives them a competitive edge over the more traditional wood and painted wood signs.

A good plastic sign is not cheap, however. So it's important to get the sign you want at the price you can afford. However, when you get into plastic signs, the businesses are often more sophisticated, and the firm may have a sign artist on staff to help you. If so, by still getting three estimates from different sign companies, you can get three artist opinions and ideas, too, and decide which one you like best. You may not have to hire a freelancer in this case.

Signs that don't fall in the above three categories are in my miscellaneous category. They range from metal letters like banks traditionally use, to signs formed by molded cement. Most larger sign companies or architects

Signs

can tell you about this sort of signage . . . and what the costs would be.

Electric lighting can also be incorporated into signage. However, many towns and cities have restricted the use of flashing and scintillating lights because they fear their city will look like a mini Las Vegas. The sign company you work with should be able to tell you what's legal and what's not.

When plastic signs were first developed, someone got the idea to put up a blank plastic panel and fit it with removable plastic letters. Thus, the first plastic readerboard was born. Today, even portable readerboards are available that can be rolled out when you're open and rolled back inside when you're closed.

The idea was great. A changeable message display along with your regular sign to enhance *Neighborhood Advertising*. It's a way to sell different products and services and *add selling detail* to an otherwise simple advertising form. For the cost, the addition of a plastic readerboard to a sign is a worthwhile expense.

Trouble is, in order for changeable signs to be read, they have to be changed on a regular basis, usually everyday. And changing those little plastic letters on a sign 10 to 20 feet off the ground is difficult and tedious. Wind can blow letters off, leaving only a portion of the message. And vandals can make surprising new words out of the letters that you used.

Another consideration is aesthetics. A large, white plastic panel leaves a lot to be desired when it comes to enhancing the architectural beauty of your building and the surrounding area. Especially when it cracks or needs

Signs

cleaning.

So, the age of electronics solved the problem. By incorporating an arranged panel of lights and controlling them with a computer or similar device that forms words with the lights, the Electronic Message Center Sign was developed.

There are many advantages to this type of "electronic readerboard." 1. It takes up less space and is more aesthetically pleasing. 2. You can change messages on the control device inside your office like a typewriter, instead of manually putting up letters outside. 3. You can put more messages up easily because it rotates words to form a complete thought. 4. The changing lamps are attention-compelling and attract greater interest.

True, these signs are more expensive than plastic readerboards and consume more electricity. However, when you weigh the greater convenience, aesthetics and effectiveness of these electronic message center signs, the relative advertising value is much greater. Most larger electronic sign firms offer lease plans to make such signs more affordable.

If you still want to use changing lamps to attract attention but can't afford a full electronic message display, consider a changeable time and temperature lampbank incorporated within your sign. Financial institutions have used these types of electronic displays for years. In fact, people refer to these types of signs as a public service . . . and often consider them a "landmark" when they give directions. "Just turn left by the bank's time and temperature sign and you won't miss it."

With any electronically-changeable display or sign, I recommend a maintenance plan so your burned-out bulbs are replaced on a consistent basis.

A few years ago, there was a panic in the electronic sign industry when sales were being affected by the dramatic rise of electricity costs. So new signs were developed that did the same thing as the electronic message and time and temperature displays, only with reflective fluorescent discs that flip to create the message.

I would carefully consider the differences in effectiveness and energy costs before I purchased this alternative form of electronic changeable sign. If your electric bill turned out to be $150 less with a "reflective-disc" display, the savings may not outweigh the sales that the electric lamp display pulls in.

New electronic sign technologies are being developed all the time. Some of them have the ability to put both typestyles and graphics on the same panel. Find out what is available in your area and compare each one's advertising effectiveness for yourself. Be sure to judge them in a driving car. That's how most other people will see them.

Remember that, just like any advertising, the medium is only as good as the message you put on it. If your messages are interesting and you change them at least once a day, people will look forward to what your sign will say. If you get lazy or put up messages that people don't care about, you'll lose their regular readership . . . and be very disappointed in the type of results you get from your sign.

No matter if you get a simple painted sign or a super-duper electronically-changeable message center sign, don't be afraid to spend a share of your advertising money on it. You'll be able to utilize the concept of

Signs

Neighborhood Advertising to its fullest and take advantage of the prospects it attracts.

And if you still are wondering if signs do any good, ask a real estate salesperson. With a sign on every property he sells, he's carrying the power of *Neighborhood Advertising* to the limit. And it works.

The typical worker today has to learn, process and respond to 24 times more information than he or she would have just a decade ago.
— *Focus*

Chapter Twenty

Reaching Your Prospects through the Mail

Every business gets mail. Sometimes a lot of it. And when you get a lot of mail, there's always weeding to do. After all, you can't read *everything* . . . and you probably don't want to.

So you begin to sort the junk from the semi-junk mail. Have you ever stopped to think about why some of that mail ends up in the "keep and read" pile while the rest of it ends up in the circular file? Well, if you ever consider doing any type of advertising mailing (called Direct Mail in the industry), that question is a darn good place to start.

After all, if no one opens your letter in the first place, what good is all the stuff you prepared inside? Not much.

Let's think about the psychology of the appearance of your envelope . . . the first thing your prospect sees. What turns you off?

Well, I'm highly suspicious if it's addressed to

Direct Mail

"Occupant" or "Homeowner." If I get "Manager," "Owner," or "President" in my business mail, that's just about the same thing. Right into the garbage. I figure if they can't put my company's name and my name on the list, it's got to be pretty general stuff.

Does it have an address label or is it personally typed? (Or at least look like it's personally typed?). That usually makes a difference to me.

Next is the "look" of the envelope. If it's got any kind of selling message on the front of it like "Now, a breakthrough in meeting planning," or "The Copier that Doesn't Copy them All!", I get the message all right. Unless I don't get any mail that day, it probably won't get opened.

The same type of giveaway is often the company's logo or address. If "Poor Veterans Life Insurance Co." appeals to you, you'll open it. But if you see who it's from first, you probably won't.

Last, the real giveaway that sends it straight into the incinerator is the "too good to be true" offer. I just won a Million Dollars? A trip to Hawaii? A Free Camera? *Give me a break, okay?*

Why talk about this stuff? Easy. If these things prevent someone's message from reaching my eyes . . . and maybe yours, too, then they are things to avoid when you do an advertising mailing on your own.

First, where do you get the names? If you're only going to mail a hundred pieces of mail or less on a local basis, I'd advise you to create the list yourself. Use the telephone book, a local manufacturer's guide or any other type of reference material you can get your hands on. If your reference material doesn't give you names and

Direct Mail

titles, take an hour or two and call the places on your list directly and *get* those names and titles. Your response rate will increase dramatically.

If you plan on a larger mailing of one hundred or more, then buying a mailing list is in order. Chances are, there's a mailing list company in your city or town. They can usually provide you with lists that can hit certain businesses, certain areas or certain demographics in your community.

Most of the time, lists are bought on a one-time basis. They throw in bogus names and addresses inside the list, so if you copy the list and use it more than once, they'll get your piece in the mail and charge you for the list again. Or worse.

The list person that runs the local mailing list company can be quite helpful. Ask him if you should get your list in zip code order so you might be able to take advantage of lower mailing costs. Or about all the postal procedures that might affect you. These people work with the post office everyday and can often give you some real short cuts.

Sometimes mailing list companies *can't* give you personalized names, but try anyway. And if you can't get personalized names, make the title as specific as you can. "Director of Engineering" is better than "Director."

Also, other places to "rent" mailing lists are from the various clubs and associations in your area . . . the Chamber of Commerce . . . industry groups, political groups, etc. They might have just the list you're looking for. Explore a little.

If you want to do a larger mailing, say to half the state or a whole region or even the entire country, a national

Mailing List firm would be the correct place to contact for the names you need. I recommend *Hugo Dunhill Mailing Lists, Inc., Edith Roman Associates, Inc.,* or *Ed Burnett Consultants, Inc.,* all of which are located in New York. I've found these firms to be very helpful on the telephone and good at getting the list(s) that I need. And at around 4 to 5 cents an address, they are not expensive services.

If you want additional help, refer to a Direct Mail list consultant. Their job is to help you find just the right list . . . and I suppose for some specialized project, their assistance is justified. But for the most part, I think that you or your agency can handle the job of getting the right list.

When you order your list, the mailing list firm will ask you what format you'd like it in: Pressure sensitive or Cheshire. The difference is this. Pressure sensitive labels are for people who put the labels on by hand. Cheshire labels require a special machine that mailing companies use to adhere the label to the envelope. If you're doing the addressing yourself, order pressure sensitive. If you're letting a mailing company handle it for you, get Cheshire.

Now that I've brought the subject up, what do I recommend . . . stuffing and addressing the job yourself or letting a mailing service do it?

It depends. If you have people sitting around the office doing nothing, then stuffing and addressing labels is a good job to do.

But if you want a lot of pieces of mail out at about the same time (say you're tying it in with a promotion on radio or TV — synergism, remember?), then I recommend a mailing service. Most of the time, a mailing service will stuff, address and take the mailing to the post office . . . all for a set fee. Some will even let you borrow their bulk rate postal number (which is a good thing to find out before you print your envelope).

If you're curious about how much a service like this would cost, figure out what it would cost you to temporarily hire enough people to do the job and how long it would take to do the job. Then, call the mailing service and ask for a quote or estimate on mailing your project. When you compare the two, I think you'll be pleasantly surprised.

So, now that you know what to do on the outside, what should you put on the inside? That, of course, depends on the type of product or service you want to sell. But there are a few rules everyone should follow:

1. *Get professional help.* Unless it's just a small mailing that you can handle completely yourself, I recommend letting your advertising agency tackle the job. Chances are they've prepared a lot of mailings just like yours.

If you don't think your agency can handle it, it's quite common nowadays to use an advertising agency that specializes in direct mail. It's usually okay to hire them and maintain your regular agency for all your other stuff.

Freelancers can also do the job, but they'll still have to be coordinated. Also, make sure both the writer and the artist have had direct mail experience before you give them the work. It's definitely a separate field in advertising.

2. *Include a letter or memo.* I strongly believe you should consider letting a copywriter write it. A properly written

letter can capture the interest of a prospect better than almost anything else. If you write it, make it the friendliest letter you've ever written. Write like people talk. And always print the letter in black ink and sign it (or print it) with a signature in blue ink. It makes the letter more credible.

3. *Include as many different pieces as you logically can.* Ever wonder why those magazine companies put a zillion items in the same mailing? They do it because they know something is going to grab your attention. They do it because it works.

4. *Make it as easy as possible for the person to respond.* Ask for the order and make it easy for the prospect to make that order. Include a toll free number. Include a convenient order form. Include a postage-paid reply card or envelope. Tell them to send no money now, you'll bill them later. The easier it is for the person to respond, the more likely he or she will.

5. *Make the outside of your mailing look as professional as possible.* I once got a letter from a Harry Maxwell. I didn't know any Maxwell, but I opened it up. It was from the manager of a large department store asking me if I wanted a credit card. Tricky. If the store name was on the envelope, I would have discarded it immediately. But I opened it up thanks to curiosity.

If you think your store name would cause a lot of throwaways, you might want to just list your address on the envelope instead. Design your envelope so that you would open it on a busy day and you've got yourself a well-addressed envelope.

Many people ask me, "what's the proper response for a mailing?" and I have to answer, "I really don't know." If you're selling diamonds for ten dollars a piece, the response could be 50%. If you're selling coal mines in Saudi Arabia, the response could be 1/100th of 1%. The response is relative to what sort of return is successful for you.

Direct Mail is one of the most precise advertising media there is, provided you get the right list and properly target your message inside. It can be very useful and inexpensive as a secondary medium in a synergistic advertising campaign.

Think about what kind of mail *you* like to get. Then design your next mailing promotion around it.

The aim of all legitimate business is service, for profit, at a risk.
— **Benjamin C. Leeming**
  Imagination

Chapter Twenty One

Specialty Advertising.

For your "matchless" prospects.

When you hear people discuss advertising, you usually *don't* hear about those offers on matchbooks for art schools or tie clips with a corporate emblem. But there's a world called "specialty advertising" that really *is* an advertising medium.

It's everything from pens to pocketbooks . . . bags to buttons . . . keyrings to calendars . . . or hats to holders. Chances are, you've got "specialty advertising" products right in your desk. See if there are any pens or pencils with company names on them. Who gave you that calendar on the wall? And what about that keyring you received when you bought that new car?

Specialty advertising is a medium in which we usually like to *be* the audience because it can mean a free gift. But what about the *advertising* side? Is it an effective way to advertise?

The theory of specialty advertising is that it continually delivers impressions of your business's logo or address as long as the item is used. Calendars last a whole year. Pens and pencils can also last a long time.

However, think about the last time you called a phone number by looking it up on the pen you were using. Or bought car insurance from an insurance agency because he gave you a keyring. Or entered that art school from the coupon inside a matchbook. I bet it's been a while.

The trouble with specialty advertising is that it doesn't work the way a lot of advertisers want it to. So, the message is often wrong and a lot less effective than it could be. Understanding the way specialty advertising works can make or break how effective it will be.

For example, you may have never entered that art school by drawing that deer or whatever, but you certainly knew what I was talking about. That's the type of awareness and name recognition that specialty advertising builds.

There are more ways to sell than just saying "buy me!" Specialty advertising sells by building goodwill in the form of a "thank you" business gift. It also sells by enhancing the awareness of the business whose name appears on the item. These are long term advertising investments that can take months or years to turn into actual sales.

So why consider specialty advertising? Because in the course of business, you end up giving little gifts and doing many of those other things anyway. So you might as well have your name on them and let those items do you some good down the line.

Specialty advertising works even better when used as a secondary synergistic advertising medium with other media in a coordinated campaign. Can you think of a political campaign without buttons, bumper stickers or other paraphernalia?

Consider using specialty advertising along with a direct mail campaign. When people get a small gift in the mail, they'll usually read what you've got to say.

Advertising tie-ins are often specialty advertising naturals. How about a logo-engraved pitcher for an apple juice promotion? Or what about all those clock radios, telephones and cameras those big name magazines give away when you buy a subscription. It's all specialty advertising.

Creativity is also an essential element in your specialty advertising success. It has to be the right item with the right message in order to work. For example, glassware that says "Use BIMBO Oil" might not be as effective as a reuseable plastic oil spout with the same message.

Specialty advertising allows you to stand out from the crowd in a variety of unusual ways. Selecting the best item to use is only the first problem. *What you say* is the second most important thing. And using an advertising professional can be of great benefit for both those concerns.

Your advertising agency should be well aware of the closest specialty advertising businesses in the area. Since specialty advertising is a commissionable advertising medium, agencies usually like the idea of doing something creative in an unusual way . . . and have developed a rapport with specialty advertising pros who tell them what's hot on a regular basis. There is a real advantage to using your advertising agency for this medium because the agency understands your firm's background, positioning and can adapt your creative strategy easily.

If you don't have an advertising agency, it's perfectly fine to work directly with a specialty advertising business. It should cost you the same, either way. Many executives in the specialty advertising industry pride themselves on their own creativity and apply it very well to their extensive line of products. In fact, since it's not usually very complicated, they often can provide any art, layout or type you might need, too . . . for a fee, of course.

Using professionals is *highly recommended* in this advertising medium, largely because specialty advertising is plagued with a lot of high-pressure telephone and mail solicitors who give the industry a bad name.

I throw away all those pen offers I get in the mail . . . even though I could get a free camera. I've known businesses to be sucked in for hundreds of dollars of specialty items with hopes of getting free trips, prize money, grandfather clocks . . . you name it.

Do not buy specialty advertising in the mail, without checking prices and product quality with your local representatives first. And NEVER buy specialty advertising on the telephone.

Frankly, once I discover I'm being pitched for specialty advertising on the telephone, I'm one of the fastest hanger-uppers around. They don't just give you an offer that you can beat almost anywhere, they take up an enormous portion of your time with their stupid pitch.

When is specialty advertising *most* effective? When it's a different application than you've ever seen before. Remember those antenna balls some service stations gave away ten or fifteen years ago? Or how about those "I

Specialty Advertising

found it" bumper stickers? Or "I Love NY" T-shirts? That was great specialty advertising.

Specialty advertising *should* be a part of your media mix, somewhere down the line. Get good professional assistance and develop your own creative item that stands out and makes people say, "Hey, that's pretty neat . . . can I have one?"

Always have enough made so that you can say, "Sure, here!" That's the type of goodwill that people will often return . . . by buying what *you're* selling, of course.

The American consumer is not notable for his imagination and does not know what he "wants."
— **Andrew Hacker**

Chapter Twenty Two

It Pays to Co-operate with CO-OP Advertising

CO-OP Advertising. You may have heard of it when a vendor or salesperson is trying to interest you in the line of products he's carrying.

The scenario goes something like this: "And if you buy our line of Wonderful Widgets, three percent of the gross sales can be used for CO-OP advertising!"

Now you might be thinking to yourself, "Hmmm, these Widgets are like the ones I have now and they cost about the same, but I could really use some advertising help. You've got your order, my man!"

And you know what? Chances are you'll never use those CO-OP dollars. Most people don't. Worse yet, a lot of people who do use those CO-OP dollars use them very badly. And wasted advertising is money spent unwisely, no matter who is paying for it.

The reason why most CO-OP goes unused is because few people really understand it. Many people feel that it is "too much hassle." What they are really saying is,

CO-OP Advertising

"I'm afraid I might make a mistake and have to pay for the whole ad."

Let's define what CO-OP advertising really is. It is a fund created by a manufacturer or distributor to encourage the advertising of the products or services it wants to promote. But it *isn't* intended to be your entire advertising budget for those products. That's another thing that a lot of businesses don't understand.

Here are some points to look for when that salesman begins talking about his company's great CO-OP advertising benefits:

1. How much does the company pay in CO-OP dollars toward an advertisement about their product? 100%? 60%? 50%? (50% is the most common).

2. Does the fund accumulate indefinitely, or does it expire every year, or quarter, or month?

3. How do you know how much you have to spend? Is it a set amount? Is it a percentage of sales? Will you get a "read-out" on how large your fund is on an ongoing basis? Is there a limit on spending?

4. What are the advertising requirements? Do you have to use certain media and certain pre-prepared advertising materials? If you create your own ad (which is truly the best idea) does it have to be approved? If so, by whom . . . and how long does it take? And will the company pay for the cost of production?

5. What is the policy toward other products in the same ad?

CO-OP Advertising

6. After the ad is run, what does the company require as proof that the ad actually ran? Does it pay gross advertising costs (so you can get your agency to place it) or does it pay net advertising costs (so you'll have to pay your agency to place the ad . . . or do it yourself).

7. How does the company actually pay the approved CO-OP advertising? By check? By billing credit? At the end of the year?

8. Will you be sent current advertising materials on an on-going basis?

If you can get answers to these questions, you're on your way to being able to evaluate whether or not the CO-OP plan is worthwhile . . . and what you'll have to do to comply with the rules and get those CO-OP dollars working for you.

For the most part, CO-OP plans are pretty reasonable. They set aside a fair amount of money, establish certain rules so the money isn't wasted and pay you for the CO-OP advertising that you do on a timely basis.

Like I said before, though, most people don't want to hassle with it. And that's a big mistake.

CO-OP dollars from one manufacturer may not add up to a whole lot. But accumulating all the programs you can take advantage of and using them together in a well-planned synergistic campaign can be dynamite!

Sure, it takes a little work. If you don't have time to pull everything together, pay your advertising agency to do it. After all, if you can do $20,000 worth of advertising for less than half the price, the coordination expense should be well worth it.

CO-OP Advertising

A lot of CO-OP plans send you pre-prepared advertising slicks, radio and TV spots, etc. They might be fine to use occasionally. But if you're creating a campaign, they probably won't work right out of the can.

Make sure you allow yourself enough *time* to 1. Develop the campaign look and feel. 2. Prepare samples of each CO-OP ad in your campaign in advance and get them approved. 3. And know exactly how much you'll be spending and how much the CO-OP funds will contribute before you purchase your media.

Like any good transaction, get the CO-OP people to approve your advertising plan and ads *in writing*. Getting approval over the telephone can mean big trouble when it comes down to who *really* pays the piper.

Another short note. Make an effort to find out whether CO-OP programs are available from the products and services you already carry. You may have accumulated a gold mine and not even know it.

The best CO-OP programs are the ones that let you design your own advertising. Then your advertising fits the image and positioning you're trying to portray.

Take advantage of your CO-OP dollars and spend them intelligently. Don't just spend them on anything that comes along to use up the funds.

When someone mentions CO-OP, find out all you can about it. It can be *a major supplement* to your advertising budget.

> *It is a thousand times better to have common sense without education than to have education without common sense.*
> — *Robert G. Ingersoll*

Chapter Twenty Three
How to Work with Printers

Almost every business needs to use a printer once in a while . . . for business cards, stationery, posters, brochures, etc. And if you work with them the right way, you'll get what you want almost every time.

Too many businesses work with printers on the "good ol boy" method, which goes something like this: "Sure, I went down to Frank's Printing to order our business cards. I told ol Frank what we needed and he said he'd put some type together and put 'em on some paper stock we'd like. He said he'd be fair about the cost and we'd have 'em by next Wednesday."

Now you might like those cards or you might not. You might like the price ol Frank charges or you might not. But one thing's for sure. If you don't like 'em, it's your own fault.

When you first decide you want to get something printed, define your job. How many ink colors will it take? What kind of paper do you want it on? Is there typesetting required and if so, what style? What is the size and quantity?

More than likely, you don't have the answers to some of those questions. But that's the first place to start.

Ask your printer for an ink color selector. You'll be able to look through the charts and pick out *exactly* the inks you want, by number.

Then, discuss the type of paper you want to use with your printer and ask to see samples of the stock. There are many choices you can make in paper selection and it's important to find the type of paper you're looking for, because it can effect the price you pay. Write down the name of the stock, the color you want, and the *weight* of the paper you want to use. In the paper industry, "Book Weight" means the type of paper that is light enough to be used in a book. "Cover Weight" means the type of paper than can be used for a cover of a book or brochure . . . and it's a lot heavier. So make sure you specify which type of weight you want. There's a lot of difference in 80 pound Book and 80 pound Cover paper weight.

If you have a little typesetting to do, ask your printer for a type chart and try to match the rest of the type as closely as possible. If you're setting completely new type, select the typestyle you like best. Then sketch out what size you want the type to be and what you want it to look like. If you can find examples, that's even better. It will give the typesetter a much better idea about what you want. Also, indicate whether you want the type *justified* (like newspaper columns) or *rag right or left* (lines that break at the closest word on the margin).

Okay, once you've gone through these preliminaries,

call at least three reputable printers in your area and get an estimate from each. Clearly specify your project dimensions, paper stock, ink colors, amount, etc.

The reason I always do this is because of the "good ol boy" syndrome that businesses and printers have used for years. Some printers, like Good Ol Frank for instance, might give you a real good price on the first job you give him . . . and then soak it to you a few projects down the way. Comparable estimates simply keep everybody honest.

Once you decide what printer to use, write-up all your specifications on paper and submit them to the printer with your job. I guarantee you this will save you thousands of grey hairs and gallons of antacid.

I issue a simple printing order that look something like this:

```
ISSUED TO:
ADDRESS:
CITY:              STATE:          ZIP:
PHONE:
SALESPERSON:
DATE ISSUED:
SCHEDULE FOR DELIVERY:
TITLE OF PROJECT:
PROJECT DESCRIPTION:
QUANTITY:
PAGES:
INK(S):
SIZE:
PAPER STOCK:
BINDERY:
PACKING:
OTHER INFORMATION:
F.O.B.:
DELIVERY INSTRUCTIONS:
COST:
BILL TO:
SEND_____SAMPLES:
SPECIAL INSTRUCTIONS:
ART & NEGATIVE OWNERSHIP OF PROJECT:
```

In this manner, I make sure everything is specified up front and written down.

Once you and your printer agree on the project's terms, the next thing to ask is when you may see a *blueline* or *photo-proof* of the project.

A "blueline" is nothing more than an image taken from the negatives that the printer will make his press plates with. So it will indicate what your project will look like on paper. It is your final approval of the project before it hits the ink, so make double sure there is nothing wrong with the blueline. If there is, bring it to the printer's attention and get it changed. If it's fine, initial it and get your project underway.

Bluelines are a good tool because there are things you can see on a blueline that you simply miss when you look at your original layout. If your printer does not use this final approval procedure, find one that does. It avoids a lot of expensive problems.

Here are some other printing terms that could be useful:

Flyer — normally a one page, 8½" x 11" sheet, printed on one or both sides.

Brochure — this can really take any shape or size, but the most common are three or four panel layouts that fold to fit in a #10 envelope, or the standard 11" x 17" layout that folds into a four page 8½" x 11" piece.

Dies — these are used in the printing world for many different applications, including embossing, foiling and stamping (cutting a piece of paper into a certain design).

Emboss — a raised print or graphic on your printed piece. This involves a special die which will add to the cost of the project. Deboss is like an emboss, only the impression isn't raised, it's depressed below the surface of your piece.

Foil — Just like it sounds, you can "print" metallic foil on paper in gold, silver and other colors with this procedure. You should always consider this process before you choose a metallic ink because it looks a lot better. A foil works wonderfully with an emboss.

Bleed — sounds awful, doesn't it? Don't worry. It only means that your ink goes to the exact edge of the page. They call it "Bleed" because the printer overprints past the edge and then cuts the paper to insure a clean look.

Serif Type — a type that varies the dimensions of lines which make up the character. This type that you're reading, for example, is a serif typestyle. Serif is easy to spot because it usually has little feet on the letters (like the typestyle used in this book). *Common serif typestyle: Times Roman.*

Sans Serif Type — this one is even easier to remember because "Sans" means without. So this type of character is "without serifs." *Common typestyle: Helvetica.*

Duotones — a two color process that gives a black and white photograph another color within its tones. Hint: Use earth tone colors, not blues, greens or reds, for best results. The subtler, the better.

Color Separations — the process that breaks down the colors of the photo or picture you want to print into four basic printing colors . . . Magenta (red), Yellow, Cyan (blue) and Black in a negative format. Your printer uses the correct negative when each color is printed and your photo or picture is re-assembled on paper. Hint: When taking photographs intended for color separation, use 100 ASA (or lower speed) slide film instead of prints.

Naturally, as your printing jobs get more complicated, you'll have to know more about printing. And since this is not a book on printing, I'm just scratching the surface when it comes to making sure your printer delivers what you are paying him for.

Using an advertising agency has its advantages in this case because there should be someone at the agency who understands the printing business inside and out . . . and will make sure you get what you need.

Treat your printer like you would any other business vendor. Spell out in writing what you want and make sure you personally approve the blueline (or whatever format your printer uses) before your project is printed. Then, if something does go wrong (and in the printing business, things often *do* go wrong), you'll have written documents and approval signatures to fall back on.

Make sure you carefully inspect your printing order once it's finished. Look beyond the first few pages on the stack. Sometimes printers put the best ones on the top of the pile and hope you won't see the inferior ones until you accept delivery.

No one likes to bother with details when they don't have to . . . that's an element of human nature. But I'm convinced it was the printers who encouraged the "Good ol boy" system we talked about. After all, who wants to print jobs over?

Don't get the wrong impression. I *like* most printers. I admire their work. Most of the time, they are a real pleasure to deal with.

Remember that good fences make good neighbors. Perhaps in the same respect, well-written printing orders make good printers. Specify your job carefully and you'll probably always have a good relationship.

An idea is the most exciting thing there is.
— *John Russell*

If we watch ourselves honestly, we shall often find that we have begun to argue against a new idea even before it has been completely stated.
— *Arthur Koestker*
  The Act of Creation

Chapter Twenty Four
Logo Lament

Your logotype, commonly referred to as a *logo*, can be vital and significant. It can virtually be the heart of your advertising program. In many cases, though, a logo is simply useless. Or worse, even damaging to your image.

In simple terms, a logo is a symbol that represents your firm's image in an abbreviated manner. It is a tool that your company can use to make a statement, usually in some form of advertising. A logo is meant to communicate your firm's name, image and positioning in a design so simple that your audience will be reminded of your firm's name, image and positioning *every time* they see your logo.

But not many logos do that, do they? In fact, out of all the logos developed in the world, only about 15% really work. I believe, however, if they don't do that job, they really aren't worth having around. Bad logos are extra baggage.

The trouble with developing logos is that most people use the wrong criteria. Instead of creating a logo that satisfies the *Name, Image and Positioning* (NIP) criteria I talked about, many people just want something that "looks nice" or "is clever" or "looks professional."

There's nothing wrong with any of those things. The trouble is they're just not enough.

Good logo development can cost money. Sometimes a lot. But if a logo is designed to satisfy the NIP criteria, it's worth its weight in gold. Most of the time, it's not an easy task.

The first thing to understand is that a logo designer *should not* be the only creative person who works on your logo project. A marketing person who understands your NIP should also be involved. Some logo designers do have a feel for marketing, but overall, their strongest talents are in design.

Businesses that use only a logo designer often end up with a beautifully-designed symbol that means absolutely nothing. I've sat in meetings before where the corporate executive said, "I know it doesn't mean anything now, but we'll *make* it mean something!"

"Let me get this straight," I thought. "You're going to advertise your logo so that people will understand that this meaningless design represents your company?" Sounds incredibly foolish, doesn't it? But even huge corporations make this tactical error once in a while.

Here's the best test you can give your logo. Show it to someone you don't know and let him guess who you are and what business you're in. If he gets it right, chances are you're in the top 15%.

When I refer to a logo, I'm not just referring to symbols. Most of the time, it's a good idea to somehow utilize your business name in the logo itself. But for your own good, don't use your firm's initials unless you want to be known by them. (Studies indicate that most people tend to confuse companies using initials for their name. And initials are often much less descriptive of what type of product or service you actually have).

Sure, there's RCA, GE and IBM. When you get your advertising budget into the billions like they have, go ahead and initialize your logo. Until then, be smart and use your descriptive business name.

Before you really put a lot of money into advertising of any kind, take a good look at your existing logo. Does it really represent the *NIP* that you want?

Changing a logo is expensive. Not just in the development, but in all its applications, such as signs, stationery, etc. But if it gets down to the difference of creating a logo that works versus maintaining a logo that doesn't, do you really have a choice?

A good logo will make good advertising work even better. A bad logo will bog down even the best advertising.

Most companies have a real sensitivity about their logo. A lot of times, they resent any talk about changing it. But if I'm putting together an advertising program for a company, I think it's an important subject to deal with before we begin creating ads that would be better with a more effective logo.

The last thing I ever want to hear is, "How do you like my firm's logo? My wife did it!" Oh boy. Not only

Logo Lament

do I get the opportunity to insult his company's logo, I get to offend his wife, too.

Most businesses start out with the right idea. "We need a logo," they say. Most of the time, however, they don't really know why. They just need to have one to be a real business, I guess.

Your logo, used properly, should be the seed of your entire business advertising image. It's a serious matter. So take the time and invest the money to create a logo that satisfies your *NIP*. And don't rest until you arrive at a logo that feels right to you.

You're going to be living with it a long, long time.

A good ad should be like a good sermon: It must not only comfort the afflicted — it also must afflict the comfortable.
— *Bernice Fitz-Gibbon*
   Macy's, Gimbels and Me

I think of art, at its most significant, as a DEW line, a Distant Early Warning system that can always be relied on to tell the old culture what is beginning to happen to it.
— *Marshall McLuhan*
   Understanding Media

Chapter Twenty Five

Newsletters. Another Way to Advertise

Newsletters can be an effective way to educate your market about your products or services and enhance your image at the same time.

Even though newsletters are normally linked to the Direct Mail category, I think creating a newsletter program deserves a few extra thoughts.

First, if you start a newsletter program, you should have a strategy. What do you want to accomplish? Do you want to feature success stories from existing customers? Introduce new products or services? Give tips on how to use your products or services more effectively?

Once you figure out what you'd like to say, it's a good idea to construct a format that covers the things you want to accomplish. The front page could always have a success story. You can have an on-going column inside about new products or services. A good format *will force* you to remain within the strategy that you created.

A good newsletter must be perceived by its audience as having news or helpful information, rather than an advertising vehicle. It really *is* advertising, though.

Your newsletter should be put together and written professionally. An advertising agency can do the work or you can hire freelance talent to do the job. It will carry a strong company image with it, so make sure the newsletter looks as good as your company is . . . or better.

Since a newsletter should be professionally done in order to be good advertising, newsletters aren't really inexpensive to do. Most of the time, it takes a lot of writing, photography, some illustration, typesetting, layout, design and printing before you ever have anything to send out.

To make your investment worthwhile, consider the following tips:

☐ Send your newsletter to both customers and prospects. Add names to your prospect list often. Send the newsletter to your sales force, too. In fact, it can be beneficial to send it to all your employees, just to keep them up to date about your company.

☐ Enclose a self-addressed postage-free reply card for more information. It's a gentle, effective way to solicit response. Code the reply cards with a color, so you know which issue the prospect is responding to.

☐ Ask your readers how frequently your newsletter will appear. If you miss a date, you don't want to disappoint your audience. Maintain a schedule of at least two or three a year, however, and don't stop the schedule once you've started unless you have a very good reason.

☐ Never charge for the newsletter. You'll never get enough subscriptions to pay for your expenses and the audience that drops off may be the ones you want to reach the most.

☐ To subsidize your costs, you can take non-competitive display advertising from other firms, if you have the time to sell it.

☐ Besides mailing them, use your newsletter as a sales tool for your salespeople. Let them personally hand them out.

☐ Make sure every library in the area gets a copy on a regular basis. You'll be surprised at the number of readers you'll reach.

After a few issues, you can begin to evaluate how well your newsletter is doing by the number of questions and quality leads that are a direct result of the newsletter. Determine if any of those leads turned into sales, too. Making money with advertising is always a good way to justify its worth.

The highest form of newsletter advertising flattery is when non-customers and unknown prospects call up your firm and ask if they can be on your mailing list. Put 'em on, pronto!

Newsletters can be effective if written and produced properly. I don't recommend doing newsletters yourself on your typewriter or computer because they just won't turn out the way you want them to. And they won't get the results you want.

Develop a good format, use professional help and stick with the program for at least a couple years. Chances are, you'll build a lot of goodwill along the way . . . and that's never hurt a sale, has it?

Good Media relationships are earned through honest, helpful news service provided in an atmosphere of mutual respect and candor.
— **Scott M. Cutlip and Allen H. Center**
   Effective Public Relations

News is what someone somewhere wants, everything else is advertising.
— **Lord Northcliffe**

Chapter Twenty Six

How to Write a Press Release

Every business needs to issue a press release now and then, even if it is just to announce new employees or career advancements in the newspaper.

Now, it's true: Press releases are not really advertising. But I've never been able to find any good advice published that tells you exactly how to write a press release that won't automatically be tossed in the circular file. So here goes.

The simple fact of the matter is that the newspaper you send your press release to is probably not biting at the bit to see your story and rush it into print. For a release to be printed, it *must* have news value of interest to at least a segment of the newspaper's audience.

1. Give the job to somebody who can write. Someone with a background in journalism is a good candidate. A poorly-written press release is difficult to understand or use. That means extra work for the editor. And that

violates the whole primary strategy of preparing a press release that will be printed, namely, *Make it as easy as possible to use.*

You see, if the press release can be "popped into" the newspaper's or magazine's regular article system, you've got a greater chance of seeing it in print. If it's tough to re-write, it will most likely be discarded for something easier to use.

2. Use your nicest, largest pica-print typewriter and type the press release on plain white bond paper or your letterhead. What? No special Press Release Letterhead? Sorry. I think it gives the appearance of a self-serving commercial, which is not a good idea.

3. Look at the samples at the end of this chapter and faithfully follow the format. Journalists are peculiar animals. If it *looks* like news in the style that they're accustomed to, they'll use it. Use wide margins so the editor can edit or add to your story if he wants to. A 55 space margin, centered, is recommended.

4. Almost always, write **Immediate Release** in the upper left hand corner. Most stories don't have date restrictions. If you end up with a press release that shouldn't be printed until a certain date, indicate *when* it *can* be released in this same area.

5. Under **Immediate Release,** place the contact person who is knowledgeable about the story. If that person is difficult to reach, use someone else. An editor may only make one attempt to call.

6. Write a headline that appeals or relates to the com-

munity somehow. That indicates to the editor that your story may have some news value and worth.

7. Limit the front page to a good headline and one or two short paragraphs. This gives the editor plenty of room to write in copy changes, typesetting instructions, etc. A good press release is two to three pages in length. End each page (except the end page) with a centered **(more)** at the bottom.

8. Continue on the following page with an upper left hand corner heading of the subject and page number. News style for writing page numbers usually looks like this: 2-2-2-2-2 (for page two).

9. Use short paragraphs. They can be edited easier on the layout table. Try to organize your release so readers know what the story is about right away, then introduce the less important details and specifics in order of importance.

10. If possible, use quotes. Quote your manager. Quote yourself. Get an "okay" in writing from whoever you quote prior to sending out the release. Quotes make a press release *much more powerful* and authentic, which means a better chance for publication. Use no more than two to three paragraphs of quotes per person.

11. Don't put your quotes together in your release, if possible. Write copy in-between pertinent to the event. A good release should have a comment near the beginning, in the middle and close to the end.

12. Use different words to begin each paragraph. An

editor will spot an amateur for sure if every other paragraph begins with "the."

13. Doublespace, of course. And make double sure there are no mistakes in spelling or grammar.

14. If you can, make personal contact with the editor you send it to. You can usually accomplish this on the telephone, but when you do, make *sure* the editor *understands* why your press release has value as a news story.

15. Deliver an important press release in person. If you can't, send it in a way that will be noticed, such as Postal Express. And even if the editor says he'll "do a story on it and don't bother with the press release," write it and send it anyway. Chances are, he'll use your release, at least for the facts and quotes.

16. If you want to provide photographs, use 8" x 10" black and white glossies. Type up a picture caption on a white piece of bond paper, fold it across the photo and tape the back side to secure it. Don't forget to put "For further information, please contact:" on it as well, in case your photos get separated from your story.

17. Always end your release with a centered **—30—** *or* —###—. It means that your story is over.

18. If your press release contains a lot of facts or data, consider adding a Fact Sheet at the end of your release. Fact Sheets can be quite useful if, by chance, a reporter takes an interest in your story and wants to follow-up with more information.

How to Write a Press Release

Remember, getting your story in the newspaper or magazine depends on making it *as easy as possible* for the editor to use it.

If you talk to an editor on the phone or in person, be courteous. After all, there's no law that says they *have* to print your press release. They don't really even have an obligation. What they *do have* is an audience that has an endless appetite for news. A well-written, nicely-prepared press release could be just what the editor is looking for.

Use the sample press release pages below as reference.

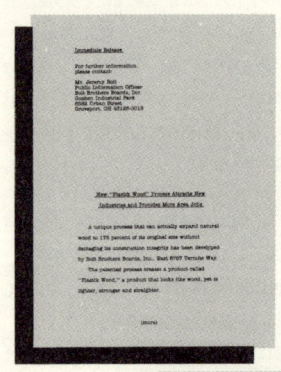

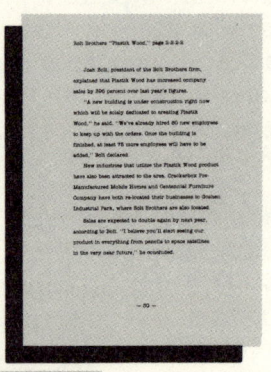

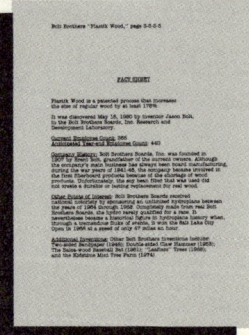

Taste is anarchy. Rules are meant to help you see the paths, but the directions are not written in stone.
— *Grace Gorichon*

Chapter Twenty Seven

Creating Unconventional Convention Displays

I've been to a lot of conventions, product shows, etc. as both a participant and an exhibitor. And I've seen companies so ill-prepared, I often wondered why they were exhibiting at all.

Like any other form of advertising, I believe you have to stand out from your competition in order to capture attention. In this case, it's important to stand out from all your neighboring exhibitors.

Unfortunately, most exhibits look the same because they rent the same tables, chairs, carpet, extra lighting, ashtrays and all the other booth necessities from a company that provides such things. Sure, it's convenient. But it makes your booth just like all the others.

Renting your furniture at a convention is not a cheap proposition, either. And a lot of times they run out of items and can leave you without, even if you ordered it in advance.

If you're going to a convention, start out by figuring the rental cost of all the items you're going to need. Then see if buying is more practical. It usually is. Even though you'll have extra shipping to worry about, chances are you won't have to wait as long as the "renters" to set up and your booth will be ready long before everyone else.

I can't tell you *how* to design your booth. That's a custom job that's different for every business. But once you've made the decision *not* to rent, you can begin to create that *unconventional* booth I'm talking about. Talk to an artist or interior designer and see if they might have some input. You might consider hiring a person to come up with a unique booth design that still satisfies your promotional needs.

People are attracted to clean, uncluttered dynamic booths. Think about the booths you stopped at the last time you were a convention participant.

The look of your booth either enhances or detracts from your company image. So it's worth it to spend a little money and time to make sure it's going to be good. Also, make sure your booth design can be easily assembled. A lot of times you *have* to use a union to assemble your booth and you want to keep those costs at a bare minimum.

Signage is important. Don't depend on the cheap sign you get for free at the convention. It looks like everyone else's, remember? Have a quality sign made that represents your logo and adds to the attractive qualities of your booth.

Other tips:

Convention Displays

1.) I prefer backlit transparencies over plain large color prints. The color just seems to be a lot more alive.

2.) If you use a video presentation, keep it short. A person passing by will watch for no longer than two or three minutes, so try to keep your story about that length.

3.) Bring back-up tapes, just in case something happens to your original. One video tape recorder will run more than one television . . . and if you have a large booth, you might want to put two or more TVs in strategic places. I recommend buying and bringing that type of equipment, too.

4.) Most of the time, you can rent "cages" that can be locked and secured after you leave your booth at night. If you have anything that could grow legs, like your video equipment for instance, rent a "cage" and use it religiously.

5.) Many companies don't adequately plan for the amount of promotional material that's required at a convention. You end up giving a lot of it away. It's that simple. So plan on it. If your promotion piece is too expensive to give out in mass quantities, create an inexpensive handout. But don't let someone who is interested in your products and services get away without information and a way to buy. Running out of business cards is also a sin.

6.) Some conventions are *buying conventions*. Some are not. If participants are coming into your booth to buy, make it easy for them to do so. Create a quiet closing booth so that your prospects can get out of the noise and

Convention Displays

convention hubbub for a few minutes. Have refreshments available in the closing area. Have your contracts ready. Special pricing and other convention specials seem to work very well.

Most people come to conventions to see the new lines, complete their business and then discover what the host city has to offer. Let's face it, after a few hours, most participants are tired and want to leave. By giving them a chance to sit down, take a load off their feet and relax, your chances of a good sale are a lot better.

7.) Make sure you have enough sales personnel in the booth at all times. There will be empty periods when you'll have a lot of employees standing around. But when it gets busy, you'll be happy they are there. Prospects will leave rather than wait to be sold. Can you blame them?

8.) Don't sit in a chair at the booth. You look too passive and will give the appearance that you simply don't care if anyone comes into your booth or not. If you have to rest, get some tall stools and use them occasionally. Chairs are for customers.

If you plan to attend the same convention next year, check out the best booths and apply for those spaces as soon as you get back to the office. Many times companies that exhibit year after year at the same convention protect their "booth real estate" and the key booths are simply not available. Make sure you have a lot of alternative booth requests in mind and you'll probably better your booth location the second year.

Dare to be different at your convention and you'll be noticed. Once a prospect enters your booth, make it easy for them to get information, see what you have to offer and to buy. An unconventional convention booth may be more difficult to create, but it's your ticket to a successful and profitable exhibit.

Research is the process of going up alleys to see if they're blind.
— **Marston Bates**

Chapter Twenty Eight
Avoid a Romance with Research

When someone says the word "research," I get really uncomfortable. I guess I've had enough unpleasant experiences with research for research's sake to make me a little jumpy.

Don't get me wrong. I'm a strong proponent of proper research on products or services to be advertised. I also advocate doing research on the competition and the way they advertise, and it's important to determine audience demographics through research . . . and to research the proper media to use.

What *gets my goat* is the way most research is conducted and interpreted. People fall in love with the positive results and are blind to all the negative factors it reveals. And that kind of romance is dangerous.

Most of the time, research is done for the wrong reasons. It is done to justify an existing point of view. And that is not the open mind that research requires.

Research

Ever wonder why even the biggest companies make notoriously stupid mistakes, even after months of study, surveys and research? The answer is simple. They asked the wrong questions and ignored the complete story.

Who would have thought that a mega-corporation like Coca-Cola would have made a formula change without assessing every possible angle and consequence? I'm sure their surveys and research indicated that there would be a minimal amount of resistance to the changeover. Why were they wrong? Easy. They asked the questions that produced the answers the management wanted to hear. Some survey.

This scenario is more commonplace than you might believe. When a business conducts a research study, they are looking for something that will indicate a benefit or an advantage over the competition in the marketplace.

A questionnaire can very easily be written in a slanted manner. "Would you say that JIFFO low-fat imitation butter tastes a.) 10 percent better than butter? b.) 25 percent better than butter? or c.) 50 percent better than butter?" Survey results? Over 60 percent of the respondents agree the JIFFO tastes 50 percent better than butter!

Now this is a little exaggeration, but it's a good example of what really does go on in a lot of research and surveys. And then the facts (if you can call them facts) are twisted even more in an advertising claim.

When a major coffee brand claims their coffee is 99% caffeine free, that leaves one percent caffeine in the coffee still, right? Just how much caffeine is in regular coffee, anyhow? See? You don't know. You just accept it as a benefit.

The problem, as I see it, is that misuse of advertising research has somewhat poisoned legitimate and fair methodology. How would anyone know the difference?

Research is still a valuable tool to be used in marketing and advertising, as long as you make *sure* all the goals and methods are honest. Be prepared and willing to accept the unfavorable comments and conclusions that research delivers, as well as the positive facts and results. And set up systems to *do* something about the negative things you've learned, instead of ignoring them and accentuating the positive.

If more businesses did that with their research, the studies would be a lot more valuable. And then maybe I wouldn't get the shivers when someone says "research."

There are two other aspects to research I think should be addressed when talking about advertising: Test marketing and Focus groups.

I like test marketing. To me, it's the most cost-effective and realistic way to test what could probably happen when a product or service is introduced to a marketplace with normal advertising support.

Many people might say in a research study that they'd like to try a non-tobacco cigarette, but when *actually* faced with the decision to buy a pack, the story might be different.

Personally, I would take the results of test-marketing a lot more seriously than the findings of an opinion survey any day.

However, you'll notice I said *normal* advertising support. The biggest mistake companies make is over-saturating the test-area with advertising. How many times

Research

have you seen huge full page ads for a product you've never seen before . . . or picked up free samples of the product on the street . . . only to discover that this product is being tested in your area?

It's simply not reasonable to compare how that product will do nationwide with test market results *unless* it's given the same extra advertising support. Most of the time, the advertising conducted on a national level is far less extensive than what the test markets were subject to. And that's wrong.

Use a fair approach to test-marketing and you'll get fair, useful results in return.

Another research aspect is a *focus group*. A focus group simply means getting a particular set of people in one room and asking them for their opinion on a prepared set of questions, which involve and concern your business or market. Often discussions spring up from the pre-set questions which reveal even more valuable data.

Focus groups are beneficial only if the "fair approach" is used. If your questions are slanted, the research will be worthless. As you can probably imagine, it's best that an independent service handles this job. I don't even think your advertising agency should conduct the session if you ask questions about advertising and image (which you should). The chance is too great that tender spots will be avoided and you will get tainted results.

As valuable as focus groups can be, the results you gather from them must be put in perspective. Keep in mind that focus groups produce data that is usually more negative than positive. Since the sample of opinion is normally quite small, a focus group provides indicators rather than cold facts. The indicators can lead to facts if you conduct repeated focus groups (at least 2 or 3 sessions) and obtain identical conclusions.

Focus Groups are especially useful in determining the Top-of-the-mind awareness order of businesses, products or services. If you end up close to last on the list, it is an indicator that you have an image problem.

Good research can save you from drilling a lot of dry holes. It can make your communication plan more defined and can target your message more accurately.

But the company that constantly researches and never advertises is just as bad as the company that advertises and never does research.

Plan for research. Budget for it. Give it a time frame and deadline far enough in advance to incorporate the results into your advertising. Valid research will yield credible, tangible results that should truly benefit your advertising.

A romance with research can be dangerous. But if you keep the relationship strictly platonic, you'll go a long way in increasing your advertising investment's chance of success.

You can't make a baby in a month by getting nine women pregnant.
— **Researcher on crash projects**

A new idea is delicate. It can be killed by a sneer or a yawn; it can be stabbed to death by a quip and worried to death by a frown on the right man's brow.
— **Charley Brower**

I passionately hate the idea of being "with it." I think an artist is always out of step with his time. He has to be.
— **Orson Welles**

Chapter Twenty Nine

Advertising: The Challenge of Blazing New Trails

The only thing constant about advertising is change. In our fast-paced technological society, our lives are affected by thousands of factors every day. Events affect us. The economy affects us. Science affects us. Even the media affects us.

And you are a different person this morning than you were yesterday.

Is it any surprise that advertising has to continually change in order to be effective? What worked yesterday may not work tomorrow. That's because the audience that responded to the advertising may vanish.

In the early 1970's, American car manufacturers kept making cars the way they *perceived* the buying public wanted: Big and inefficient. However, events like the oil crisis and strategies like planned obsolescence, the American buying public had changed. Smaller, gas-efficient foreign cars became more popular. Even though

The Challenge of Blazing New Trails

American car manufacturers *increased* their advertising, their message was still the same. And people weren't buying it.

The big-car audience simply wasn't there anymore. Detroit had to change its whole advertising approach — *as well as their product line!*

Not only can your audience change, but your advertising media might change, too.

Not too long ago, AM radio ruled the airwaves. The medium demanded premium radio dollars because it had the audience to support it. But as more and more people began to tune into FM radio, AM lost its market share. Now the roles have reversed and FM is king of the hill.

Many people feel they can bundle up the things they know about advertising their products and services and use a tried and true theme and methodology over and over again. It's just not that way.

Every advertising campaign has a rated life. It begins rolling, achieves momentum, peaks in efficiency and then declines.

Coke is no longer the "Real Thing." Pepsi doesn't "Pour it On" anymore.

Advertising is like a lock that automatically keeps changing its own combination. You have to keep figuring out new ways to turn the tumblers if you want to keep opening the lock.

That's the challenge of advertising. Every new concept attempts to anticipate who your audience will be, where it can be reached and what it will react to.

Some business people have a natural feel for what will be hot. But most rely on their advertising agencies or consultants to come up with advertising that is in tune with the audience they want to reach. The logic is that people in advertising spend a lot more time studying the changes in media and social attitudes, so they are better equipped to create an effective concept.

Your advertising should blaze new trails to reach the people you want to reach. If your ad is just like something that's been done before, you're taking a chance that the audience hasn't changed. And in today's world, that's a big risk.

There's no such thing as "safe" advertising. If you take an ultra-conservative advertising approach (and take few chances), your advertising will largely be ignored. You'll pay for your mediocrity in the lack of results.

If you aim for new horizons, you might occasionally miss. But the rewards of hitting the hot spot of your audience should justify any attempt you make.

Advertising that is fresh contains a lot of energy. People pick up on its energy and carry it around. They may talk about it or write articles about it. Even joke about it. And it gets results because it penetrates the protective barrier we erect to avoid being so easily influenced.

Why does it penetrate that barrier? Because it's something we've never seen before. It's something for which we couldn't prepare our defenses. Fresh advertising takes us by surprise and captures territory in our brain.

Before you begin your next advertising campaign, think about how you can freshen-up your concept and approach. Ask your advertising agency for its input or hire a consultant to give you a new view on your advertising situation.

Don't settle for advertising that is just "okay." That's the way your audience will react to it.

It's important to understand why your advertising needs to be continually updated, so *you* can make sure that it *gets updated*. It's your responsibility. Not your advertising agency's.

You have to be the one that wants to do great, fresh advertising. You have to be the one to communicate this desire to your advertising agency so it *can* develop solutions. You have to be the one who has the courage to use an advertising concept or an approach that's new.

Advertising agencies will tell you that great advertising is a cake with a lot of important ingredients: positioning, facts, concept, creativity, intelligence, media buying and production. But the most essential ingredient to great advertising is a great client. One who is aware of the need to continually create fresh advertising and has the courage to do so.

If you want your advertising to *really* work, don't let it stagnate. Realize that the world is constantly changing and that your advertising has to change with it if it's to work.

No one said it was easy, either. It takes a lot of sweat to create advertising that isn't a rendition of the tried and true.

When the solution is discovered though, your advertising will carry along a little of the extraordinary.

Until your competition catches up, the new trail you have blazed will be yours alone.

> *Imagination continually frustrates tradition; that is its function.*
> — **John Pfeiffer**

> *Every new idea is obscure at first. It is or it wouldn't be new.*
> — **Robert Irwin**

Chapter Thirty

Knowing Enough to be Dangerous

If this had been an advertising instruction manual like *How to do Layout and Design in Five Easy Lessons* or *Mastering the Art of Advertising*, you would truly know enough about advertising to be dangerous.

Advertising can't be instantly inhaled or shortened into a *Reader's Digest* Condensed Book. Many of the fundamentals of advertising are in a state of evolution.

In fact, advertising professionals virtually spend their lives learning and practicing their craft. So that's why I *didn't* write a book like that. It would be like sending you up in space and giving you only a flashlight.

But this book should better equip you for the systems that already exist in the real world. A lot of them aren't perfect, but they're a lot better than attempting to create advertising completely by yourself.

In a way, this book *will* make you dangerous. You won't be intimidated by media salespeople. You won't put up with an advertising agency "yes man." You'll have the tools to know whether or not your media space and time was bought correctly. And *lots more* advertising self-defense.

It's a book that should help you become a great client, even if you do work for yourself in-house.

I don't know all about advertising. Far from it. The truth is, I'd be afraid of someone who says he knows all there is to know about the advertising business.

I try to learn something new about my craft every day. Since advertising surrounds us, it's not hard to find places for new ideas. Like video taping commercials on TV. Recording radio spots. Cutting ads from magazines and newspapers and saving them in a file. And you can do the same thing. The nice thing about advertising is that the latest stuff is happening *right now*. Instead of tuning advertising out, tune it in . . . and formulate what you'd like your advertising to be.

I'm not a fan of copying ideas. Originality is one of the most powerful factors of advertising. However, if a good ad or commercial can "inspire" you to a new concept, it simply served as a stepping stone.

That could explain why advertising people enjoy studying advertising that other agencies create.

There's no secret to the resources they use. Two of the most popular advertising magazines are called *Print* and *Communications Arts* and you'll find copies of them at almost every agency in America. *Creative Review*, from England, is another good magazine.

You should subscribe to at least one if you like to keep up on the latest trends. They're not all that expensive and make nice "coffee table" books for your living room or for your front office reception area.

Examine those resource materials carefully and see how advertising professionals *simplify* complex ideas and concepts. Someone once told me that a good idea had to be short enough to be written on the back of a business card. When it comes to advertising, the simpler you make your message, the easier it will be to understand.

Trim the excess fat from every advertising message. It's always worth the struggle.

For almost every business, advertising is a fact of life. But because so many business owners don't understand its nature, it's treated with nonchalance.

Armed with the knowledge that this book contains, you *can* take control of your advertising destiny. You *can* work within the system and get results. And you don't have to know all there is to know about advertising to promote and benefit from great advertising.

Remember that advertising isn't an expense — it's an investment toward a profitable return.

Hire the people who can do your advertising best and make sure they do their finest work. That's *your* job. Doing anything less could be fatal.

> *There are advertisers, some of whom are large and important, who are suspicious or fearful of the unexpected nature of a real advertising idea.*
> *— John E. O'Toole*
>   *Chairman*
>   *Foote, Cone & Belding*

Radio Splash Theory: Waste Demographics; Egomaniac Syndrome; Greed Syndrome; Unspecific Syndrome; N.I.P. — Name, Image & Positioning; and Neighborhood Advertising are trademarks of Edmond A. Bruneau/Creative Consultants.

The office of Edmond A. Bruneau can be reached by calling (509) 326-3604 or by writing to:

                Edmond A. Bruneau
                P.O. Box 9909
                Spokane, WA 99209-9909